whiteasparagus

Collected Works
by D.R. Belz

To Judy—
Best wishes!
Enjoy the book.
Dave Belz

white**asparagus**

Collected Works
by D.R. Belz

D.R. Belz

with an introduction by
Rafael Alvarez

Baltimore, Maryland
www.apprenticehouse.com

Copyright © 2010 by D. R. Belz

Library of Congress Cataloging-in-Publication Data

Belz, D. R. (David Richard), 1956-
White asparagus : collected work / by D.R. Belz ; with an introduction by Rafael Alvarez. – 1st ed.
   p. cm.
Includes bibliographical references and index.
ISBN 978-1-934074-53-4 (alk. paper)
I. Title.
PS3602.E4635W48 2010
818'.6–dc22

                    2010018551

Printed in the United States of America

First Edition

Cover concept and photo by Doyle Partners, New York.

Author's photo by Jim Burger.
Photo location courtesy of The Howard Rawlings Conservatory.
Book design and typesetting by Sheila Watko.
Typeset with Champagne & Limousines and Baskerville.
Printed in the United States of America ISBN: 978-1-934074-53-4

"And Little Lambs Eat Ivy" from "Mairzy Doats," words and Music by Milton Drake, Al Hoffman, Jerry Livingston. Miller Music Corp., NYC, 1943.

Published by Apprentice House
The Future of Publishing…Today!

Apprentice House
Communication Department
Loyola University Maryland
4501 N. Charles Street
Baltimore, MD 21210

410.617.5265
410.617.5040 (fax)
www.ApprenticeHouse.com
info@ApprenticeHouse.com

For Muz.

"'And I do love a newspaper. You mightn't think it, but Sloppy is a beautiful reader of a newspaper. He do the Police in different voices.'"

—Charles Dickens

Our Mutual Friend

Table of Contents

Stories

Foreword

The Real & Imagined Worlds of D.R. Belz

"When I was a boy, the moon was a pearl, the sun a yellow gold.
But when I was a man, the wind blew cold, the hills were upside down . . ."

- Tom Waits

That good old world over which Waits is crooning in a melancholy waltz was glimpsed by a boy through a chain link fence behind Northbourne Road in Baltimore's Northwood.

Nose through a wire diamond, fingers hooked through the holes, the kid glimpsed the last of the old world pass by before it vanished in a 1960s blur of avocado green Frigidaires, Tupperware parties, and bell bottoms.

"When I was six or seven, this old guy would come through the neighborhood every so often ringing a school bell, and it sounded ominous. He looked like a seedy St. Nick. He could have been Father Time, for all I knew," remembers David Belz.

"He wore a shabby leather coat and pants. He had a white beard, like Shirley Temple's grandfather in *Heidi*, and he carried a big brown wooden box on his back."

He was, Belz would learn later, the knife grinder.

"The wheel was in the wooden box on his back, and I only saw one woman on our block come out to give him knives to sharpen.

"I would crawl under the junipers along the fence to catch a glimpse as he walked by. He probably never even knew I was there."

A hyper-literate, wise-ass Catholic kid (he began writing science fiction in the third grade and counts *Mad Magazine*, Monty Python, and the Society of Jesus as influences), he learned one, simple truth:

"'Someone is always crazy, but when two are, it's worse.'"

And so, from up and down that alley and the world he discovered beyond comes this collection of satiric essays, poetry, and short stories.

A *D.R. Belz Reader*, some 30 years in the making...

And if the knife grinder didn't notice him, no matter. For a mere ten years or so later, the noir novelist and screenwriter James M. Cain [1892-1977] did.

"I was 16 years old and had written a long short story inspired by a bunch of Orwell I'd been reading. (Richard M.) Dick Prodey, one of my mentors at Loyola High School, entered it in a statewide literary contest," said Belz. "It won.

"So I went to College Park that summer and lived in the dorms with the other young literary aspirants. At the time, I had no idea who one of our teachers, James M. Cain, was. He was eighty years old then, and when we came in the afternoons we'd find him asleep on the couch in a rumpled business suit with his legs tucked under him.

"He said things like: 'Good writing is writing done for money' —because that was how you knew it was worth something. And: 'Girls shouldn't hitch-hike.' This was 1973, remember. One girl jumped up and called him a sexist, but Cain just looked at her and didn't say a thing. Of course, he was right."

And time, it seems, has proven Cain right about Belz as well.

The old man left a message for Belz on the flyleaf of *Cain x 3*, Cain's 1969 collection of the novels: *Mildred Pierce, Double Indemnity and The Postman Always Rings Twice.*

It reads: "To David Belz, who gave me a glimpse of the future that frightened me —in the hope he enjoys it . . ."

That future is one that perhaps only one of Belz's heroes—Swift, Poe, Twain, Thurber, and Mencken among them—would recognize.

That one is Kurt Vonnegut.

In *Slaughterhouse-Five*, Vonnegut feared a future "according to General Motors." Today Belz labors to make sense of one delivered each day by media conglomerates across the country that continue to make writing for a living harder and harder.

This is a present-tense future in which outlets for the written word —never more devalued by Cain's yardstick than in the first decades of the 21st century —are at once infinite and scarce.

Many of the prose pieces in *White Asparagus* originally appeared in newspapers, on which the plug will soon no doubt be pulled; and literary magazines, most of which no longer bother to send even form rejection slips.

Like Hollywood, you simply hear nothing.

Nothing at all.

"There's very little room in newspapers for news anymore much less the stuff that I do," said Belz. "But if you see me out in the yard walking the dog, it's because I'm trying not to write."

Here's a moment of gratitude that he didn't try too hard.

—Rafael Alvarez

Macon Street, Baltimore

Thanksgiving, 2009

Acknowledgments

I am indebted to dozens of people who had a hand in making this book.

I am grateful for the love and support of my family. Thank you to my wife Rena; my children Mary Eleanor, Grace, Claire, and John T.; and to the Belz, Mudd, and Nehrling families. And thanks to Muz, Constance O'Toole Belz, who has never failed to ask me how my writing was coming.

Thanks to my generous friends: Rafael Alvarez for an introduction. To Jim Burger for the author's photograph. To Stephen Doyle of Doyle Partners in New York for creating the design concept and photograph for the cover.

Thanks to my teachers and mentors for their patient inspiration: Richard M. Prodey, Michael Iampieri, James Johnson, Robert Keller, Bob Cullen, S.J., Sr. Maura Eichner SSND, Phillip McCaffrey, Thomas Scheye, and many others.

Thanks to the editors of the publications who first saw fit to put my work between covers: *Unicorn*, *City Paper*, the *Valley Times*, *The Evening Sun*, *The Baltimore Sun*, *The Baltimore Examiner*, the *Southern Literary Messenger*, *Oregon Review*, *Antietam Review*, *MacGuffin*, *The Cynic* and others.

Thanks to the writers and colleagues who influenced this work by their example and their encouragement.

Thanks to all of my students, who taught me everything I know about teaching writing.

Finally, thanks to the publishers, editors, and designers at Apprentice House Press who believed in and encouraged this project: Lauren Hooper, Marguerite Pravata, Sheila Watko, Gregg Wilhelm, and Kevin Atticks.

—D.R. Belz
Chestnut Ridge
Spring, 2010

The following program contains scenes of
graphic violence, adult language, and nudity.
So, what are we waiting for?

Going Metric, Going Crazy

Now that there's a well-established European Union, you can bet that sooner or later the specter of the United States converting to the metric system will rise again.

But I don't care what they say. I don't care how many public service commercials they produce. They might be able to tax my income, regulate my driving, standardize my deductions, approximate my demographic make-up, optimize my consumer-producer potential, as well as take all of the hormones out of my beef jerky, but no government in the world is going to make me "think metric."

They can't make me think in meters, kilograms, liters or Celsius. I like thinking in the English system. I speak in English. I write in English. Why can't I walk, lift, drink, and even sweat in English?

I've heard that the metric system is logical, accurate, and scientific. Above all, it's systematic. Well, therein lies the downfall—and the beauty—of the English system. It's entirely chaotic. Two pints to the quart, four quarts to the gallon, 36 inches to the yard, 5,280 feet to the mile—this wonderful non-system glories in whimsy, in arbitrariness.

It seems to me the world is a lot like that—fluid, unpredictable, inaccurate. The indiscriminate English system of measurement is perfectly suited to this, the most indiscriminate of all possible worlds.

While government and business might conspire to change my monkey wrench into a metric spanner, force me to fill up my gas tank with liters of gas, and establish that a trip from Baltimore to Ocean City, Maryland is 243.2 kilometers, I can rest with the knowledge that they will never succeed in purging our language of the poetic, albeit unscientific influences of the English system.

After all, what other name for a hogshead but its own? How else does an engine run but on horsepower? Five hundred sheets of paper is nothing other than a ream. A score of something? Why 20, of course. A dozen is 12; a kindly baker makes it out to be 13. I've given my body strict instructions: When I give blood, it is to stop at a pint—none of this liter stuff.

If something is incredibly heavy, it weighs—not a metric ton—just a plain old ton. Horses are hands high, their reins feet long. They run not kilometers, but furlongs. Football players fight for yardage. A country mile is substantially longer than a stone's throw; a city mile is 12 blocks, a block being what you fancy.

My shirt size is 36 long in inches; my neck size is 16 of the same—just keep those crawly centimeters off my body. If you've ever chopped a cord of wood, you know exactly how much it costs in calories, those magical quanta responsible for shedding ounces and pounds. It would take a meat ax to take of a kilogram, I'm sure. When sailing, you look to do knots, not kilometers per hour. Our clothes are made from bolts of cloth, measured in yards, to be sure. And I've never missed having an accident by a millimeter, but by a hairsbreadth.

Most official rhetoric on the change to metric emphasizes that the United States is the last industrialized nation yet to switch over to the metric system. Even the English, they tell us, have abandoned the English system.

Since when has the United States done anything sensible just because everyone else is doing it?

I say, let's force the rest of the world to be poetic, backward, and unsystematic.

Let's make them use the old feet-yards-miles and see how they like being force-fed some kind of foreign conspiracy.

Let us not budge in this weighty matter—not one iota! Let inefficiency reign! Long live the square acre!

The Joy of Cooking Internationally

With this, the all-new, sixth edition of *The Joy of Cooking Internationally*, we extend our sincere wish that a world of fine eating come your way!

We hope this volume will allow you to appreciate what the various ethnic groups have to offer the true gourmet of cuisine international: their varied temperaments, from those spicy Latin dishes (chapter 12) to those salty New England chowder heads (chapter 9), as well as their attitudes toward your desire to serve them—in their own natural juices, which, incidentally make excellent soups and stews (chapter 3).

Don't miss such tempting world-famous favorites as Swiss Steak (page 23) Blacks' Eyes Peas (page 345), Jewish Wry Bread (page 67), Chilean con Carne (page 112), and a delicious Turkish Taffy (page 98).

Finally, we hope this book will give you new ideas on serving the people whose guts you've always hated, but never knew how to prepare. Bon appétit!

The Editors

The Joy of Cooking Internationally

Irish Stew

2 cups potatoes, peeled and cubed

2 cups carrots, chopped

1 cup onions, diced

1 hod peat moss

1 large Irishman

2 fifths cheap whiskey

Wash Irishman thoroughly in strong disinfectant. Place in cold oven with whiskey and allow to marinate. Remove bottles and set oven to 325 degrees. Place vegetables into a large pot of boiling water and simmer for thirty minutes. When a fork leaves clean holes in Irishman, remove from oven and chop—and don't ye be talked out of it! Add Irishman to vegetable stock and simmer 'til the cows come home, or about two hours. Serve on paper plates and garnish with a pinch of damp peat moss.

Baked Alaskan

1 yellow cake mix

1 quart vanilla ice cream

3 cups fresh fruit

1 fresh-frozen Alaskan

Thaw Alaskan for forty-five minutes in the 'fridge. Clean, bone, and skin. Track and shoot a wolf from a helicopter and make oven mitts from its hide. Bake yellow cake in a greased sheet pan according to package directions. When cool, cut in four inch squares. Place thawed Alaskan in blender and set on "chop" function for six minutes. Top each cake square with Alaskan, ice cream, and fresh fruit. Warm in 225 degree oven, about four minutes.

Scotch Broth

pot of boiling water

1 Scotsman

Prepare one large haggis according to the recipe on p. 76 and then discard. Render Scotsman down in boiling water. Skin off fat and reserve. Save bones for soup. Ladle into dishes and serve piping hot with croutons and warm ale.

German Chocolate Cake

2 tsp. vanilla

1/4 lb. melted butter

1/2 cup sugar

4 eggs

4 cups flour, sifted

2 cups chocolate, semi-sweet

1 German, medium size

Trick German into taking his clothes off by telling him it's time for a shower. Salute German and pin a medal on his chest, if desired. Place in food processor and puree, about six minutes. While humming "Ode to Joy," slowly pour German puree over flour, sugar, eggs, butter. Melt chocolate with a flame-thrower. Fold into mixture. Grease two nine-inch round cake pans with an Italian's head. Pour batter into pans–don't spill!–and bake at 400 degrees for one and a third hours *exactly*. Remove. Allow to cool thoroughly before icing.

French Fries

cooking oil

16 ounces dry Chablis

salt and pepper

4 good-sized Frenchmen

With great finesse, heat oil to 400 degrees. Untie, clean, and slice Frenchmen into one-inch strips. Float slices in a dry Chablis for twelve minutes. Season to taste and place strips in oil, retreating from the spatter, as needed. When they float, they're done! Drain on absorbent paper and serve on either side of the plate, as a side dish, or by themselves on celery.

Noodles Romanov

2 pounds fresh egg noodles

1 cup diced onions

2 cups sliced mushrooms

a member of the Romanov family

Prepare noodles according to package directions. Sauté onions and mushrooms in butter. Dance around the kitchen with the Romanov and get him or her staggering drunk. Pound with a wooden mallet until tender. Sear in a large frying pan and slice when brown. Add three tablespoons cooking sherry to sautéed onion and mushrooms. Add slices of Romanov. Simmer mixture twenty minutes, stirring occasionally. Drink half a bottle of cooking sherry, then pour Romanov and sauce over well-drained noodles. Serve by candlelight with balalaika accompaniment.

Boola, Boola!

I have just now stopped laughing at the news that episodes of "I Love Lucy" have been inadvertently reaching what exobiologists think are extra-terrestrial intelligences in our neighboring star systems. Yet another news report says our star neighbors are going to be treated to a very deliberate and expensive broadcast of the Yale school song, "Boola, Boola." The scientists behind the project think the song is friendly sounding and harmless.

It is.

But while we are about the business of broadcasting friendly earth say-ings, I think we should consider these: Yabba-dabba-doo, Yippy-yi-yo-kiyay, Hootenanny, Yankee Doodle went to town, and so on.

I think it's a little late to try to think up anything profound to say to our star neighbors, if they are, in fact, listening. Because if they are listening, they already know all about us. Nothing we can say now can ever recover Lucy's "Ethel, do I have a plan!"

I'm sure Lucy, as our first interstellar ambassador, has explained every-thing to them, and yet has told them very little about us.

Certainly, they would now rather fly their light ships into the Gravity Cauldrons of Amber Arcturus Nine than land on our little world and an-nounce their arrival like Michael Rennie in the original *The Day Earth Stood Still.* (They shot him, remember?) Without a doubt, on their star charts, three dots out from Sol, is a little red flag on a pin. To any inquisitive traveler of this part of the galaxy, the flag says "Beware: Earth."

And that explains it all, and explains nothing.

I have a suspicion there's a maxim in use out in the big blue universe that has been recognized everywhere, like American Express.

The maxim is: "Speak, for heaven's sake, when you're spoken to."

Most three-year-old children on earth learn this advice as a matter of casual etiquette, but somehow retain only a very vague sense of the precept.

In the same way, Earth is one of the little children of the universe; we babble and squawk and pump out megawatts of disorganized radiation molded to the shape of our minds, interstellar maxims be damned.

We are somewhat egotistical in thinking that every capable intelligence out there is beating a path to our little mote. Even the Thumb People of Orb Cycle 49 think of Earth as some sort of practical joke invented by their radio astronomers. If intelligences have been receiving early television signals for years, they have better sense than to blunder into our missile sights.

There used to be a wonderfully effective TV commercial (perhaps our star neighbors have seen it) of a crowd of people in a stadium, watching a tennis match. One man mentioned that his broker is E.F. Hutton, and E.F. Hutton says— and of course the entire paid attendance and the players turned to listen. Wouldn't it be nice if all the universe were like that crowd, and good old Earth like the unwitting fellow in the midst of it, ready to say something of cosmic import?

Imagine the surprise of our star-friends, if they were so whimsical as to train their ears to Earth and hear the last, frustrated strains of "Boola, Boola!" when all we meant to say was "Hello, how are you?"

Your Astrological Forecast

Virgo

August 24 to September 23

Impose your values on an ambivalent person. Taurus individual will not see things your way; go to lengths to convince this person. You are a dominant personality. Influence small children to become bilingual. Do not take no for an answer. You are immortal.

Libra

September 24 to October 23

Evaluate your options. All is not lost. Do not throw stones at glass houses; get off the fence; take a few risks. Take life easy; speed things up. Knock off early; stay late. Eat out; eat in. Use butter; use margarine. Sit down; stand up. Go to sleep; wake up. Make friends; get lost.

Scorpio

October 24 to November 22

You will have an accident. Learn to talk without using your hands. Don't be tempted to strike out on your own. Success is transitory. You can't take it with you. Do not ask for whom the bell tolls, it tolls for thee. Farewell to arms.

Sagittarius

November 23 to December 21

Venus is in your seventh house. Jupiter is in your lunar house. Obama is in the White House. You are in the dog house. There is smoke in your chimney, snow on your eaves, water in your basement, and all your chickens have gone to roost. Return to the womb.

Capricorn

December 22 to January 19

You have erotic fantasies about sharks. You will have more than a casual relationship with a war-surplus vaporizer. Suppress your desire to imitate mummies. For a good time, call 1-900-555-8000.

Aquarius

January 20 to February 18

Someone in a car will ask you for directions. Check the soles of your shoes before traveling extensively indoors. A man with two teeth will vituperate your person in Esperanto. Someone will ask you to examine her mica collection; be diplomatic.

Pisces

February 19 to March 20

if u cn rd ths, u tw cn hv an xcting creer in mtchbk cpy edting.

Aries

March 21 to April 20

Beware oversized snowshoes. Do not take syphilitic Berbers into your confidence. Expect serious repercussions from a decision to invest in a sort of organic transistor. Synchronize your watch. Mars is in your lunar house: some will give you a doughnut machine.

Taurus

April 21 to May 21

Don't take any guff from a loudmouthed Virgo: get physical with this person, if necessary. You are correct in thinking that everyone with an apostrophe in his name is a socialist. Someone close to you will attempt to get you to eat poison. Accent on ballistics.

Gemini

May 22 to June 21

Some people tell you that you possess a charismatic personality; they want something. You are considered to be a boring chess partner. Demand your own lifestyle: eat with your fingers.

Cancer

June 22 to July 23

Be cautious of dirty money. You will notice that one of your ears is lower than the other; remedy this. Chew your food thirty-two times. Accentuate the positive. Your mother reads *The Congressional Record* for the racy parts.

Leo

July 24 to August 23

There is nothing in any of your houses. It should not surprise you that buses and taxis will not pick you up; a lint brush would refuse to pick you up. This portion of the zodiac has been discontinued. May your cusp wither and drop off. Raspberries.

TM

I'd like to be a fly on the wall at the annual convention of the International Trademark Association. It's a group I had initially assumed must be made up of high-powered lawyers closely connected to the Association of People Who Put the Little Round Stickers on Every Piece of Fruit in the Grocery Store.

The INTA, founded in 1878, is actually an organization that just wants us to observe good grammar. They even publish a media kit so that writers and editors will understand the rules of trademark use and, through a kind of trickle-down marketing, educate the public on the importance of trademark names.

The big danger, they tell us, is that because of misuse by the public and writers, trademark words are in jeopardy of falling into everyday use. And if a trademark word is used unprotected often enough in the common parlance, if writers use it uncapitalized as a common noun without the necessary trademark symbol, it may cease to be private property and become, well, just any old word.

You'd think product-makers would be falling all over themselves to turn their products' names into the garden-variety term for a given product. It's all a little like getting dressed up to go to a singles bar, only to keep telling everyone you meet how happily married you are.

The folks at INTA do make a couple of interesting grammatical points. One is that trademarks were never intended to be nouns at all, but rather adjectives that carefully describe a generic product or service name. For example, you should say, "Oops, I just spilled sulfuric acid all over the Formica brand laminated-plastic countertop," instead of saying, incorrectly, "I think I just trashed the formica."

In addition, you should never pluralize trademarks. Never use them in the possessive form and never, ever, use them as verbs. This means you would never write: "Jim was chased for several blocks for his new Nikes." Or, "My Rottweiler loves to chew Pizza Hut's boxes." Or, "I need to Xerox my resume."

Certain former brand names have, in fact, fallen into everyday use, including aspirin, cellophane, cement, dry ice, dynamite, escalator, kerosene, laser, linoleum, margarine, mimeograph, nylon, shredded wheat, telegram, trampoline, yo-yo and zipper.

A few words—never protected by trademarks to begin with—have vainly struggled to preserve their unique identity in the face of impostors; take champagne, for instance, or potato chip.

Avoiding unwitting trademark abuse is practically impossible because, according to the INTA itself, what you might think are some rather dog-eared words are actually trademarks.

For example, if you send your kid's teacher a note saying that the Band-Aid adhesive bandages all over his shins are from taking a pair of Teflon non-stick fluorocarbon resin spikes in the shins at Little League Baseball practice, you may get a Post-it self-stick note back stuck to the Velcro hook and loop fasteners on his Windbreaker jacket requesting you apply some Vaseline petroleum jelly to his scrapes and get him to take up Rollerblade in-line skating or better yet, Ping-Pong table tennis.

After some fairly Saccharin sweetener thoughts about sending a Xerox photocopy of this saucy reply to the school principal, you opt instead to raid the Frigidaire refrigerator-freezer for some Jell-O gelatin or a Popsicle flavored ice.

Just then, your Realtor real estate broker, who is anxious to sell in your Zip Code mail coding system, parks her Jeep all-terrain vehicle and comes walking up the front walk, trips on a Day-Glo daylight fluorescent color Hula Hoop plastic hoop you thought you had long ago pitched in the big Dumpster trash container down next to the Laundromat self-service laundry.

She vaults backward into your Fiberglas fiber Runabout boat, bumping her head against the Plexiglas acrylic plastic windshield. You play the Boy Scout rescuer, take her a Kleenex tissue and some water in a foam cup (INTA says cups are not made of Styrofoam plastic foam), just as your dog bounds up with her empty Rolodex rotary card file like a Frisbee flying disc in his mouth.

See what I mean? While trying to get by without brand names can be virtually impossible, life with trademarks for most of us can be just one big Rollercoaster amusement ride.

The Million Monkey Room

Report to the Senate Appropriations Committee re: FQ4 2008.

Senator, I appear here today to testify on why Congress must refrain from cutting funding for the Million Monkey Room Project. As you know, the Project was a research initiative funded as an add-on provision to the recent Economic Stabilization Act of 2008—otherwise known as the "Wall Street Bailout Bill." As you recall, this provision was justified by the Committee for both strategic and national security concerns.

Our project's goal was to prove the often-quoted saying: Put a million monkeys and a million typewriters into a room, and at some point, one of them will type out Shakespeare. The thinking was that—if feasible—this technique could then be applied to other texts of strategic importance to the country.

It worked.

I am proud to report today that our project has achieved historic results.

In fact, on October 6, 2008, one of our simian charges, Monkey #671,876 typed out a near perfect First Folio version of *Hamlet*. Of course, no extraordinary breakthrough is without its kinks, and this one is no exception.

The "Foggy Bottom Hamlet," as we have dubbed this manuscript, unfortunately, lacks the letters "l" and 't' throughout. For a reason we are still investigating, Monkey #671,876 simply did not use those two keys at all in the text. Undaunted, our team of handlers is standing by, placing dabs of peanut butter on those two keys at Monkey #671,876's typewriter.

At any rate, here's an amazing sample of this history-making text from Act III, scene iv after Hamlet accidentally kills Polonius in Queen Gertrude's closet and tells her of Claudius his uncle's vile crimes. Her response, according to Monkey #671,876?

"O Hame, speak no more:

hou urn's mine eyes ino my very sou;

And here I see such back and grained spos

As wi no eave heir inc."

The Million Monkey Room next tackled—at the request of Congress—several more test projects of national security importance, including The Constitution of the United States (Sadly, the simian typist on the project, Monkey #143, inadvertently left out the Fourth, Sixth, Twelfth and Fifteenth Amendments; we don't see as this as fatal flaw, however, unless someone reading closely at Justice notices the omissions.)

In addition, at your request, the Million Monkey Room typed valiantly around the clock the dozens of pages of text for the recent Economic Stabilization Act itself. Admittedly, because of time constraints, they could not get all the provisions into standard English, which is why some of the Act appears to be written as Euclidian geometric postulates, a lost Cajun dialect, and a form of Mayan haiku.

But despite this dedicated service, the Million Monkey Room Project now verges on insolvency. Today your Committee moves to slash The Million Monkey Room's appropriation, contending that our funding was somehow a "pork barrel" mistake.

We question this, since from the beginning, the Project was designed to be self-sustaining. The Million Monkey Room was scheduled to begin work on a number of historically and culturally useful texts, including the New Testament, the Koran, and the Talmud in their entirety; *The Joy of Cooking*; the Los Angeles County Yellow Pages; and every song ever covered by Nat King Cole.

Granted, we could not have foreseen this quarter that global markets for recycled monkey scat would collapse, leaving the Project with no way to generate supplementary self-funding. On the contrary, we ended up with tons of material we could not unload on the markets—having had to store it in the basement of *The Congressional Record* offices.

We will leave you with what we clearly see as our only alternative to keeping the Million Monkey Room operating absent continued federal funding. Our three-part solution, while workable, is dire, and certainly not the most desirable:

—Sell off the entire Room of one million monkeys to online political blog sites.

—In their place, employ one million GS7 grade government workers.

—Sell shares in a privatized Project to the Book of the Month Club.

The choice is yours, Senator. We await your decision.

Do your duty.

Hand Jive

As an urgent matter of public policy, Americans need to learn to talk better with their hands.

Italians, of course, have long been the experts in the art. And if you've been watching the news coverage from the Middle East, you know that Arabs and Jews dialogue with their hands famously. (Strange that they don't get along better.)

In our own culture, people who digitally dialogue well include TV meteorologists, quiz show models displaying prizes, the guy on the airport tarmac with the earmuffs and batons, and, of course, sports referees. But necessary professional hand-talking aside, Americans tend to be woefully illiterate with their hands.

We have, if you will, a "hand jive gap."

When was the last time you saw two people really going at in public, gesticulating and working the air between them? We're not talking American Sign Language here, either.

Sure, we all can talk with our hands when we absolutely *need* to, like when we order four hot dogs, three beers, and nachos with cheese at the ballpark. Hands also blaze when people get cut off in the car, racing someone else to the next red light.

But why do Americans suffer from such a general hand-vocabulary malaise? We sent a man to the moon forty years ago, but we can't make ourselves understood in a loud, crowded cocktail party?

Notoriously bad hand talkers, Americans are more finger-lingo handicapped since everyone had give up smoking and found they needed something to do with their hands. Bored digits cried out mutely for some employment. And you can only chew so much gum.

So we invented cell phones and text messaging.

Now we can do something in public that looks almost as cool as smoking and probably still gives us about the same amount of cancer— only more slowly and on only one side of our brains. You can walk along and talk to someone you're going to see in about fifteen minutes anyway, but you just wanted to say "Hey" to. Or, you can browse through the online movies, rattling off titles to your partner because you *better* not download another dog like the re-make of *The Day the Earth Stood Still.* Or you can look like you're putting together an important business deal at your kid's soccer game, when actually you're listening your voicemail from people you saw about fifteen minutes ago who just called to say "Hey."

But what has caused this digital linguistic gap to begin with? How did the Russians, for example, get so far ahead of us in talking with their hands and owning overpriced neighborhood grocery stores? The answer is simple: Americans have been underexposed to the art of speaking with their hands.

I propose that we Americans take the time to rediscover hand vocabulary and to talk more with our digits. Here is some basic hand language to get started on the path to speaking clearly.

1. *"I'm telling you the truth; believe it."* Take five fingers of one hand and point them together in a wedge, like your trying to pick up a grain of cooked rice. Then, drive the point of the wedge into the outstretched palm of the other hand like a bird pecking seed. Hold this up in front of the face of the person you are speaking to. (Rice and birdseed are optional.)

2. *"I'm not having any of that."* Hold the of both hands palms up, facing out, and wag your hands back and forth as if you are wiping condensation from the windshield of your SUV. Do not do this while driving.

3. *"You and I think much alike. We are simpatico."* Point your elbows out, put your hands in front of you, thumbs up and palms facing your chest, one in front of the other. Then, like a Ferris wheel, rotate your palms around one another, creating a circular motion. Move this manual vortex up and down for emphasis. Do not do this near the court during a professional basketball game.

4. *"I understand. I am in agreement."* Form a circle with the thumb and index finger of one hand and splay the other fingers out in a fan. Raise this circle to eye level and bounce it in the air three times. Since a European will probably punch you when you call him or her this body part name, only use this gesture *inside* the U.S.

5. *"That makes no sense. You are crazy."* Point the index finger of one hand at your temple and draw quick circles in the air. Alternatively, tap you forehead while extending your tongue out the corner of your mouth. Then be prepared to execute #2 above, quickly.

Finally, remember, if you want to erase the hand sign you just gave someone, touch the bill of your cap, drag your hand across the letters of your jersey, and vigorously rub your forearms. Failing that, a good shrug should do just fine.

What Things Cost

Some things in life cost way more than you'd expect.

I'm not talking here about the nine dollar and fifty cent hospital aspirin or the cost of any part even remotely associated with your automobile's exhaust system.

The cost of those things is, of course, absurdly and artificially inflated because of what economists call *prevailing market conditions.* This is the fundamental right of hospital administrators and car dealerships to charge you ridiculous prices for inexpensive things because you are a consumer and, well, who really knows what a car muffler costs, anyway?

And I'm not talking here about the difference between brand and so-called "generic" products. Of course, we're all used to the idea that you pay $16.99 for a pound of Hawaiian coffee and $3.99 for a pound of something in a white can with black letters that appears to simulate "ersatz" coffee of World War II and may even be war surplus—who knows?

What I'm talking about are those things priced all out of proportion with what they are made of and the labor it took to make them.

Take example, the simple set of snack trays. A couple of strips of wood, screws, and a coat of lacquer, right? The cost: forty or fifty bucks. Oh, sure, they probably make the things out of *gopher wood* from the island of Malta, or something.

Remember that big chunky set of carved wooden salad bowls and utensils you got as a wedding gift? Again, forty or fifty bucks. Could they be made of —perchance— gopher wood?

And what the heck is *gopher wood* anyway? It's probably common cypress, a fragrant and fairly waterproof wood they once used to make coffins out of. It's the wood that legend tells us was in the shafts of Cupid's arrows. Why? Because it lasts forever. And when God told Noah to build the Ark, the specifications called for —ah-ha!—gopher wood!

So let's not even get into those carved chess sets, saltcellars and pepper mills, humidors, shoe trees or patio tiki torches. (Gopher wood, anyone?)

I think you catch my drift: there seems to be an international conspiracy to fix the prices of certain suspicious consumer items. It is not at all surprising that these items frequently turn up as both wedding gifts and garage sale merchandise. Consider, too, that they all have one peculiar thing in common: they are things you might only own once in your life.

Think about it. How many sets of snack trays have you ever owned? How about lobster traps? Ouija boards? Bat houses? Four woods? Cranberry rakes? Mortar and pestles? Bongos? See, not that many. Are these things not made from —*et voilá*— gopher wood?

And just take a look at that little carved wooden box you have from someplace like "Sea Isle City, Nebraska" into which nothing will fit. They're like bellybuttons; everybody's got one. Cedar? Not likely. Try *gopher wood!*

To review, then, here are the characteristics of these objects that international pirates probably have sweatshops full of manacled carvers cranking out by the millions:

1. You will probably only ever own one of them.

2. They cost on average forty or fifty bucks.

3. They are made out of gopher wood.

Be on the lookout for these items; they are passed among us. How can you know them? Check the little white sticker on the bottom that tells where the item was made: No doubt, it divulges the location of an international cartel headquarters in New Jersey—or a prospering factory in a gopher wood forest somewhere on the island of Malta.

How can you avoid being taken in by this international conspiracy? Here are three guidelines:

1. Don't ever marry. Failing that, ask that all wedding gifts be donations made in your name to your favorite charity or to Save the Gopher Wood Forests.

2. Avoid flea markets and garage sales. And whatever you do, don't bid more than forty or fifty bucks on an unopened "box lot" at auction.

3. Buy plastics.

College: Not Just a Seven-Letter Word

Advice for parents of late high schoolers: If you think the college search has been stressful, wait until you pull away from the curb of your child's dormitory at (Insert name of your matriculant's college or university here).

It's not just that that they're faster, nimbler, thirty years younger, fifty pounds lighter, with darker hair, tighter jeans, and firmer skin. They live to party.

I can hear you protest: But *my* kid's different; my kid has at least the sense God gave a bunch of turnips. Unfortunately, that won't be enough. And I shudder because, well, I'm getting kids number three and four ready for college.

And if you don't believe me, just ask the presidents and chancellors of more than 125 of the country's best-known colleges and universities who've called for discussion of a lower drinking age as part of The Amethyst Initiative (http://www.amethystinitiative.org/). Or the community college president (not an Amethyst signatory) who resigned with a $400,000 severance package for drinking beer on a boat with his shirt off.

So while you're waiting for the "thick envelopes" to arrive, practice gulping down tranquilizers by the handful and consider some of these exploded myths of college experience for "newbie" parents.

Myth: Moving a child to college must necessarily resemble the Normandy Invasion. Wrong. Here's a packing tip: Wait to buy the appliances. Or you'll inevitably find your kid in one fourth of a 10' x 10' room with four big screen TVs, four DVD players, four sound systems, four mini-fridges, four microwaves, four mini-vacs, etc. You can relax because the roomies in your child's "quad" will buy their own industrial-strength blender—and not just for milkshakes, either.

Myth: As "digital natives," college kids are the masters of today's marvelous array of electronics. This one will keep you awake at night. College kid calling home: "Hi Dad. My (insert "iPod," "cell phone," "laptop," etc. here) fell into (insert "the toilet," "a blender full of kiwi dai-quiris," "a child's wading pool full of chocolate pudding"). My roommate tried to dry it out with a road flare, but it still doesn't work…Can I just order another one—*please?*"

Myth: College kids today are more health-conscious than ever. True, but only if you consider tanning and eating beef burritos after 2:00 a.m. a form of New Age religion. You may have heard that eighteen-year-olds believe they are immortal; they frequently act accordingly.

Myth: My child will not fall victim to the dreaded "freshman fifteen" pounds of weight gain. In fact, most college freshmen eventually convince their parents that they have converted to vegetarianism when, in fact, they are regularly pounding down thousands of calories in turkey wraps, chips and salsa, and flagons of "lite" beer.

Myth: My kid would never dare carry a fake ID. OK. But here is post-9/11 America's dirty little secret: Since one of their favorite hobbies is copious amounts of premarital drinking, college students accept fake IDs as a one of the facts of life at U.S. institutions of higher learning. A study published in *Psychology of Addictive Behaviors* reported that by the end of sophomore year, nearly 33% of college students surveyed reported that they owned a fake ID, a fact that ought to be giving folks at the Department of Homeland Security ulcers because the other 67% probably responded with "What do you mean by 'fake?'"

I'm not worried though; to make up for this breach of security, the rubber-gloved people at the airport have trained Doberman pinschers to sniff my shoes. I somehow sleep easier with that knowledge.

ValuesRUs.com

Shoppers! Looking for the perfect holiday gift for that person on your list who has *everything*? This holiday season, give the gift everyone's talking about!

According to exit polling in the last presidential election, moral values scored high on a majority of voters' list of important issues. "Yes," millions of voters said, "Moral values are very important to me." But we know what they're thinking: "Yes, yes, important, but where do I *get* some?"

Search no more! Now, there's *ValuesRUs.com*, your on-line moral values store—where we take the guesswork out of your holiday moral values shopping! And you don't need a Ph.D. in philosophy to get high-quality moral values and start using them right away. Heck, you don't need any education *at all*. We do all the work, so you don't have to!

At *ValuesRUs.com* we can help you figure out such brainteasers as:

- Is it OK to tell everyone that I am very morally conscious, but then raise my children without limits to their wants and chuckle when they are rude and obtuse to others?
- Is it morally wrong to teach my children a variety of curses while I tailgate people down the highway trying to be first at the next red light? What do I do at the intersection *after* I've flipped off the guy I nearly sideswiped?
- Does my investment portfolio really need to leverage sweatshop labor in Micronesia?
- How much gas should my SUV burn going down the driveway to get my mail?
- Am I morally obliged to turn off my cell phone at the symphony?
- What is the most ethical choice in hollow-point ammunition for my handgun?

Now, at *ValuesRUs.com*, we'll help solve those kooky dilemmas of modern life with our selection of fine products, each FDA-approved, tested by experts and guaranteed to be safe for children and nontoxic to the morally impaired.

Check our specials for this holiday season:

Moral Values Samplers—Three of our most popular moral values packaged in an attractive conundrum: integrity, fidelity, and veracity. Samplers are stitched onto genuine rare okapi hide using 100% infant llama wool. Framed and ready for hanging in your family room or den. (Free delivery to all red and blue states in the continental U.S., Puerto Rico, U.S. possessions, and territories in the Middle East. Made in Mexico.)

Moral Values Deluxe— This complete selection features moral values every which way but loose! Ten kilos of shredded moral values in an attractive, serviceable container made of high tensile, transparent categorical imperatives. Shake it up and look!—the moral values flutter down onto the little hand-painted reproduction of Washington D.C.—just like your favorite snow-globe. Delight your friends and confound your enemies with this terrific display of moral values just perfect for your mantelpiece, desk at work, or dashboard this holiday season. (Not available in all Zip Codes. Truck-shipped or air dropped. Some settling may occur during shipping.)

Shop *ValuesRUs.com*. You simply won't find higher quality moral values anywhere!

Plus! This holiday season, we're offering special holiday volume discounts. Order two or more of any of our moral values packages, and we'll throw in a case of handsome leatherette-covered bibles *absolutely free!*

So don't delay! Visit *ValuesRUs.com* today and stock up on *your* moral values while supplies last.

In fact, we may have run out already.

The Reader

The MacDougals had just about the best of everything imaginable.

They had a grand home; two bright and vivacious children (male and female they had them); two extremely efficient imported cars for work and a large inefficient SUV for play; four television sets, one of which took up an entire wall in the room of the house known as the "television theater;" three video gaming systems (one for each of the kids, Katie, 13, and Jimmy, 17, and one for Mom and Dad); and they possessed other assorted luxuries of the good life, nay, the delightful life in America in the early years of the 21st century. Among these excesses was the best professional Reader money could procure.

The Reader's name was Houston Hancock. He was 22 years old when the MacDougals hired him.

The MacDougals' Reader came every Tuesday and Thursday evening, and every Wednesday and Sunday afternoon. On every third Thursday, the Reader presented MacDougal with a bill for services, except for Thanksgiving Day, which was still a holiday in the 21st century in America, even for Readers. (This is not to say that the Reader was exclusively the MacDougals' Reader; on the other days and at other times he went to other homes, but the MacDougals, by contract, were entitled to believe that the Reader was theirs alone.)

"Mom! Houston's here!" Katie or Jimmy would say upon the Reader's arrival, and from that moment until 5:30, the Reader plied his trade in the MacDougal home, in much the same way the plumber puttered under the sink or the television man moved like a wraith behind the TV wall.

"Read this," Jimmy would say, thrusting a cereal box into the Reader's hands.

"Fortified with seven important vitamins," the Reader said, turning the box over, "Send four proof-of-purchase seals and $4.98 for your free Day-glo Astro-Frisbee . . . Contents may have settled during shipping and handling because the box was packed by a machine . . . Ingredients: sugar, high-fructose corn syrup, corn starch, dextrose, vitamin B-6 and B-12. Our product guarantee: if not fully pleased, send the remaining portion back to us for your full refund. Offer void where prohibited . . ."

"Me next!" giggled Katie, who was clutching a crumpled envelope. The Reader took the letter and opened it. He could still make out on the deckled envelope the seal of a Scribe from Pittsburgh.

"This is the letter from Granny MacDougal. I read this last time," the Reader said, and knew it was not his place to debate an assignment, but did anyway in the face of the sheer redundancy of the letter.

"Oh please, Houston!"

"Dearest Katie," he began in the measured practice of his art, "How is my littlest granddaughter? I hope you received the set of porcelain dolls I sent from Quebec on my recent trip there . . ." His eyes flitted to the bottom of the page where the old woman had apparently taken pen in hand herself to inscribe the robin's egg paper with her own signature. Professional ethics aside, the Reader felt a twinge of uneasiness at the sight of the shallow and shuddering script.

Jimmy went into the television theater and began watching a program called "Eat Your Heart Out" in which contestants battled to avoid winning big prizes on which they were obliged to pay enormous taxes. A cleanser commercial came on and a morose announcer said, "Life isn't very happy at the Joneses – They have dirty bathtub ring . . ."

Jimmy sang along with the jingle for a moment and then switched to a soap opera in which six of the minor characters had entered into an open marriage based on a bizarre credit card fraud scheme.

". . .and I am happy to tell you I enjoyed my flight to Montreal very much . . ."

Mrs. MacDougal came out of the kitchen wiping her hands on a dishtowel.

"Hi, Houston. I'll be with you in a moment. I'm sure the kids have lots for you to do."

The Reader finished the letter from Granny MacDougal, then read the afternoon program selections from the satellite TV menu to Jimmy, who was walking around and around the sofa, watching.

Mrs. MacDougal finally sat down next to the Reader with the morning mail.

"This one first," she said, handing the Reader a crisp letter.

"It's from *Reader's Digest*. According to the outside of the envelope, you could be one of hundreds of big prize winners; as a matter of fact, you may have already won the big prize."

"Oh, I've heard all about those big sweepstakes drawings. You can discard that one. How about this one?"

"It's from the Gas and Electric Company. The little insignia on the cancellation says: 'Heat happy, heat healthy with gas'."

"How about this one?" she said, holding out an advertisement for fine furniture, upside down.

Etiquette for the 21ˢᵗ Century and Beyond

Now that the new millennium is well underway, let's face it: humanity hasn't accomplished all that much, "Net, net, net," as the lawyers say. No cure for cancer; no solution for world hunger; no humans permanently living on other planets. We haven't even been able to keep water out of the basement reliably.

But some things have changed. Take etiquette, for example.

What we do for a living has become so much a part of modern life that the traditional "How do you do?" has been replaced by "What do you do?" followed close on by "What kind of hollow-point ammo does your handgun take?"

Cell phones and call waiting have made interrupting someone in mid-sentence a required social skill for the new century. Learn to practice this artfully by yelling "Whoop, there it is!" when, at the symphony, your phone starts playing Beethoven's Fifth in the middle of Brahms's Third. And when someone is explaining the details of her marital breakup, mutter quickly: "Uh-huh, uh-huh. uh-huh, uh-huh." When a friend tries to convince you that *cell, web* and *net* are all words for things that imprison us, respond with a slow, sarcastic clapping.

Tell everyone who will listen that you are very "green," but remember to raise your children without limits to their wants. If they don't wish to, your children should not be made to go to school, since this might traumatize them and make them think you don't love them enough or want to be their friend. Teach them to be independent and self-reliant, which experience shows consists largely of being rude and obtuse to others.

Teach them that no man is an island, but if you can manage to be a peninsula, you're three-quarters of the way there. Encourage them to harshly criticize people who believe everything they need to know they learned in kindergarten. In the spirit of nurturing their First Amendment rights, teach them a variety of curses while you tailgate people down the highway trying to be first at the next red light.

Marry not wisely or well, but often, which experts agree will become the quickest route to self-actualization, without having to claim it on tax forms. Remember that the reason married people live longer than single people is that misery loves company.

Live so that your grandchildren will recount the story of your life and spouses, ending it: "And so they lived happily ever after, for awhile."

Build an outrageously large, ostentatious house that will show people how good you are at wheeling and dealing, looking out for number one, being your own best friend, going for it all, and picking out wallpaper with ducks all over it. This will also show people that you know what "ostentatious" means, making them feel shallow and small.

Have a suitable guesthouse built out back for them: just under five feet tall at the eaves and about three and a half feet wide. Supply no guest parking, and don't let them wash their car at your house, either. Or maybe let them, but don't supply a hose or nozzle.

Dress so that people can see that all of your taste is in your mouth. Accomplishing this will require the purchase of clothing emblazoned with animal fetishes as trademarks, as well as the names of various foreign designers. It should all seem rather weird under the surface, and, speaking of under the surface, buy all of your underwear from stores that run large expensive advertisements of people posed nearly naked in with empty champagne glasses trying to appear as if they are expecting dinner guests.

Strive to make your life a study in extravagance. Because simplicity is the soul of elegance, simply flaunt your lifestyle to everyone you come in contact with. To soothe your guilt at living so histrionically, join a volunteer peace and justice league, but don't invite them over for cocktails.

Your hobbies should include artificial rock-climbing, closed-pen spear fishing, alpine paintball-skiing, motocross racing (desert only), and reading thick annual reports at the beach.

Your analyst's patient files should read like the social register.

Keep yourself lean and hungry by regular exercise at an exorbitantly priced health club with overtly sadistic personal trainers. Your investment portfolio should read like an antitrust case. Dabble in futures, doodle in margins, shoot the moon on suspect security-backed investment instruments, and generally make a planetary nuisance of yourself by investing in corporations involved in rapacious enterprises in the Third World.

Finally, take consolation in that, while your friends won't really like you, only diamonds are forever.

Addicted to a Naughty Habit

I'm thinking of having a card made up to carry around in my wallet, somewhat like the medical emergency cards, which will read:

"I am a cigarette addict. If you give me a cigarette, I will smoke it. If you smoke a cigarette in front of me, I will watch you smoke it. As I would like to live to a ripe old age and have lots of great grandchildren, please don't give me a cigarette or smoke nearby. Failing that, please blow some my way."

Cigarettes in movies these days aren't cool. In fact, I'm not sure they ever were. In the intrigue thriller "Winterset" made in 1936 (that was when you could still buy a $15 suit and H.L. Mencken still wrote for *The Evening Sun*) an evil character says with great aplomb, "Give me another coffin nail." He means a cigarette, and everybody in the audience shivers at that point. In "Body Heat," William Hurt jogs and smokes simultaneously, one of the best bits of character development in years. And look what happens to him.

The only people in movies who smoked and got any real respect were Garbo and Bogart, and we all know how their characters were movie paradoxes, heroes who never seemed quite wholesome or completely heroic.

Cigarettes, let's face it, are naughty. We're told that right from the beginning until we're old enough to know better, and then we're old enough to choose to be naughty. Cigarettes, unfortunately, and ironically, are a link most people have with their carefree and rebellious halcyon days. Fast cars, provocative clothes, late hours, and a pack of butts. Or, if a person never went through the rebellious stage, smoking later vicariously fulfills the need to be naughty.

I remember my first cigarette as other people remember where they were when Kennedy was shot. In the woods, a bunch of friends and I smoked a cigarette, the kind with the mysterious chambered filter. We puffed and puffed and then waited for the police. When they didn't come, we wandered off to play wiffleball, thinking we knew something we weren't supposed to, but couldn't quite figure out what.

We were warned, though. One of Perry Mason's adversaries, Hamilton Berger, played by real-life smoker William Talman, did a TV spot for the American Cancer Society that stated, "I'm dying of lung cancer . . ." We shivered, sure it was because he never agreed with Perry.

The president of the R. J. Reynolds Tobacco Company is on record as having said that the tobacco industry doesn't have much time left in this country. I believe this is probably because the decline in people's smoking is linked to the realization that smoking past a certain age ceases to be a glamorous, rebellious lifestyle and begins to be a rebellion against life. If you can feel a chill lighting up, it may well be the icy hand of death upon your shoulder.

You will note the signals if you and your friends are getting ready to quit. You begin by using each other as scapegoats. "I only smoke around you." "You're corrupting me." "I can't believe you still smoke those things – give me one will you – and don't tell." Now, we're naughty again, sneaking smokes on the back porch at parties. Trouble is, there are a lot of us on that porch. But we were warned.

They tell me that people stricken with catastrophic illness frequently ask the question "Why me?" If the TV and movie stimuli that induce people to smoke by example have been removed, and the link to heart disease and cancer is a strong one, why do people continue to smoke? Print the skull and crossbones on the pack with a big label in red stating "Poison!" and I'll wager people will still light up.

Filmmakers don't use cigarettes as a symbol of being cool or sexy or glamorous anymore. I'm not sure they ever did, really. But I can still see Rod Serling introducing the early episodes of "The Twilight Zone" ominously smoking a Chesterfield. We were warned. Why do we do it? There's a sign-post up ahead.

Next stop . . .

Smoke

"… experts now have identified a related threat to children's health that isn't as easy to get rid of: third-hand smoke. That's the term being used to describe the invisible yet toxic brew of gases and particles clinging to smokers' hair and clothing, not to mention cushions and carpeting, that lingers long after second-hand smoke has cleared from a room."

—*The New York Times*

The healthcare debate raging across America has inspired new levels of caution among doctors and medical researchers, who are worried that a) people might not have enough on their minds, and b) if true health care reform arrives, the medical profession may not have much to do anymore. So as the serious business of research into the ills of smoking and its effects continues, we'll no doubt continue to see dramatic improvements in the abilities of medical science of identify these silent environmental killers in our midst:

Fourth-hand Smoke: This is the contamination you receive if you are still storing the cremated ashes from your Great Aunt Wilma who died of lung cancer from smoking thirteen years ago. She was a grand old dame, but she sure could put away those coffin nails. And she was none too diligent about her personal hygiene, either. So yes, doctors say: Keep that urn locked up in the closet and not right out on the mantelpiece where the toxic substances might leech out into the air and onto your children's cereal.

Fifth-hand Smoke: These are the chemicals your child ingests if you simply *imagine* a cigarette burning in an ashtray in a smoking car on a train outside of Philadelphia in 1978. You remember, back before you even *had* kids. You can see it now, can't you? Hmmm, take a good long whiff! That's fine quality tobacco, right? You sure do miss *that*, don't you? You did *a lot* of things before you had kids. Get over it. Recovered memory can be hazardous to your health!

Sixth-hand Smoke: These are the toxins your kids get a heavy dose of if someone just *tells* you they saw someone else smoking somewhere. It doesn't even have to be someone who's describing it very well. And the person smoking it might be in a hurry, standing outside a high-rise apartment building or something. Keep your kids away—*and safe*—when the person telling you about the person smoking really gets down to the nitty-gritty.

Seventh-hand Smoke: This is the critically dangerous level of smoke-related contaminants your family receives if you have a *dream* about someone smoking near your house. It's smoke residue from your subconscious mind, so remember to open the windows and turn on the fan when you wake up, for Pete's sake! Break out the Lysol and wet naps.

Eighth-hand Smoke: This is the dose of radiation your infant will receive if you were to hum "On Top of Old Smokey" in the shower. Even if you have the vent-fan on, the chemical pollution from this song is highly toxic to little ones. Beware!

Ninth-hand Smoke: This is the level of chemical jostling your loved ones receive if you handle or (God forbid) actually *play* a CD of Smokey Robinson's greatest hits. Okay, it *is* a great collection, but what's more important? Your family's health or a funky stroll down memory lane with one of Motown's greats? And don't try to sneak by using headphones either! The smoke in your soul will still seep into your kids' brains. Playing the album on an iPod only concentrates the contamination.

Tenth-hand Smoke: This is the disturbing level of level of exposure you bring into your home every time you watch *Casablanca*. Particularly insidious, this contamination reaches its highest concentration when Humphrey Bogart and Claude Rains walk off into the fog at the end. And that fog? That's toxic, too, so keep the kiddies way clear of the Blu-Ray!

One last time now: *smoking kills*. What more evidence do parents like you need? Why put your kids in jeopardy needlessly? Be on the alert for these additional levels of toxic chemical pollution from cigarettes. Your child's imaginary friend's life might depend on it.

Tutor to the Stars

That morning my wife had left me for a Hollywood star. She'd been doing this for some time. She said she'd be back later that afternoon. And I was wondering why I put her up to it.

The Hollywood star was involved in homicide.

"Be careful," I said when the affair started.

"He's only 13," she said. Besides, she reminded me, he didn't really commit a homicide. He was an actor in the TV show *Homicide*, which debuted that Sunday after the Super Bowl. The Barry Levinson "Homicide." I said I'd be watching for the kid my wife tutored, to see if he blew any lines or anything.

My wife said he was very polished, that he was a good student and liked his regular school back in New York. She said his mother came to the set with him in Fells Point and was very protective.

"That's good," I said.

As a writer, one of my habits is to read the daily newspaper cover to cover, searching for interesting or bizarre stories, tidbits to spin off into plots and articles. The other people who do this are the ones who play the ponies.

It all started when I spotted an ad for a tutor. My wife was a foreign language tutor at the time, so I clipped the ad and taped it to the refrigerator door. She called the New York telephone number and talked to a company that set up tutoring services for children when they toured the country shooting movies and TV series, performing on stage and training for athletic competition.

My wife commuted to the *Homicide* set in Fells Point in the morning, and when the kid actor wasn't on the set, he was "in school" with tutors the New York company had hired. The actors' union regulations stipulated a certain amount of time each day the kid stars had to be embraced in the bosom of academe.

That evening, my wife said that as soon as her feet hit the ground from the car, she was escorted everywhere she went by someone with a headset. When she was tutoring the young star, this assistant to the assistant to the assistant director hovered anxiously nearby.

I tried to sound as if I were a party to this new-found glamour, a co-conspirator.

"I'll bet you eat very well," I told her before the first day. "That's the thing about movie sets. They always get great caterers."

I knew this because I used to write television commercials and got to sit around and yuk it up on the sets as the commercials were filmed. Food, it seemed, was something just short of a fetish for the production crews. This is probably because shooting commercial film consists of seconds of extremely tense work juxtaposed against hours of mind-numbing tedium. Eating takes the edge off.

That evening, my wife acknowledged that there had been much grazing in Fells Point. "It was amazing. I could basically get whatever I wanted to eat."

"Did you see anybody famous? Did you get to meet Barry Levinson?"

"No, but a nice, young man did come up and welcome me to the set. It turned out he is the series director."

"Did you get a chance to talk to Ned Beatty?"

"Who's Ned Beatty?" My wife spent the better part of her childhood in foreign countries, so sometimes she doesn't recognize icons of popular American culture like Ned Beatty ("Hear My Song," "Deliverance"). She can, however, regale you with interesting details about Diana of Great Britain and Caroline of Monaco. She can tell you what brand of underarm deodorant they used.

Later, watching TV, we saw a program with Ned Beatty in it.

"That's Ned Beatty," I said.

"Oh, yes. He speaks to me all the time. He's very nice."

"Yeah, well, he's famous," I said.

"Daniel Baldwin speaks to me, too," she said.

Then it was my turn to be ignorant of the famous.

"I don't know him," I said.

"He's Alec and William's brother. He's very friendly."

"What's this Daniel Baldwin got that I ain't got?"

"A hit TV series," she said.

From then on, I started to curb the urge to clip from the newspaper, unless it's for the ponies.

The Caveman Diet

Recent studies by medical researchers say that the best way to prolong our lives is to restrict our daily calorie intake by fifteen to twenty percent. Imagine somebody keeping cages of cranky, middle-aged mice on low-calorie diets until the mice could fit into the shorts they wore on their honeymoon. That and forcing them to watch the Chuck Norris Total Gym commercial repeatedly.

But how can we ordinary humans benefit from this amazing research? Sure, you've tried the low-carb diet, the Beverly Hills diet, the French Women Don't Get Fat diet, the Israeli Army diet, South Beach diet, Weight Watchers, Jenny Craig, NutriSystem, Slim Fast, Medifast, even Weight Loss 4 Idiots. But nothing seems to work, right?

A better diet is to imitate our prehistoric ancestors in the forests primeval. Contrary to most fast food menus, our primitive ancestors were not dietary cretins. Their secret was called the Caveman Diet. It's deceptively simple: Eat only what's immediately available in the forest. This includes many nutritious things such as wild fruits and vegetables, nuts and seeds, eggs, fish and shellfish, berries, leaves, bark, flower blossoms, mushrooms, truffles, snails, insects, tree sap, and wild honey. Anything *readily found in nature.*

Can you eat pancakes on the Caveman Diet? No! Pancakes require a) an artificial heat source, b) a non-stick cooking surface, and c) a batter mix not readily found in nature.

Granola bars? Good question. While granola bars are indeed compressed slabs of honey, nuts, whole wheat or oats, and raisins, they are manufactured and extruded through machinery that you would not be able to find in the woods. So the typical caveman would not find modern granola bars in nature.

What about doggie treats like Snausages? Same deal.

How about chocolate syrup, you ask? No way. Chocolate syrup is full of high fructose corn syrup—again a processed product derived from fructose, corn, and syrup, three things not readily found in nature. Think: tree bark and acorn husks. Think: newts and grubs. Think: raw shredded wheat without the frosting.

What about a fish fillet sandwich? Are you kidding? You have to catch the fish, ship it from the Indian Ocean to Thailand for processing, then fly the quick-frozen fish pieces to a factory in Mexico where the breading is baked on, then assemble the whole thing on a bun with a slice of American cheese from milk solids made in Australia and a blob of tartar sauce in your local fast-food joint. Way too many moving dietary parts. Remember: Cavemen ate only foods *readily found in nature.* Tartar sauce is definitely not found in nature.

Cucumber salad would be on the Caveman Diet, right? Yes. You could conceivably find a sharp stick to chop with, a wild cucumber, a wild onion, and some wild balsamic vinegar and sour cream to mix together in a kind of hollowed out tree bark bowl that you could place into a swift-running creek to chill for a half an hour, so yes, cucumber salad is on the menu. Now you're getting the hang of it!

Another Caveman Diet recipe? Rinse off three handfuls of ripe wild blueberries in spring water. Pat dry with some cattail fluff and mash between big rocks until smooth. Scrape the blueberry paste into a turtle shell and place on a sunny rock to warm. Flick off the yellow jackets and serve on chunks of raw shredded wheat for a delicious teatime canapé.

The trick known to all veteran naturalists and survivalists is to *sniff, lick, nibble, spit.* Pay close attention to what those guys on the survival shows eat, only without the obvious camera set-ups, rehearsals, and Gatorade breaks; what we don't get to see is their quickly spitting out that chewed up scorpion and tossing back shots of 110 proof bourbon.

It turns out, however, that most things readily found in nature are perfectly edible with some exceptions like toadstools, hemlock, henbane, deadly nightshade, cauliflower, and your maiden aunt's holiday eggplant casserole. Rest easy that most of the time, mother nature will gently warn you off eating anything that's bound to make you sick, even sushi.

So, *sniff, lick, nibble, spit*—and eat hearty, cavepersons.

Gift of the Cicadas

Recent studies are beginning to suggest that the fabled 17-year locust is really neither. Misnamed locusts for no apparently good reason, cicadas, as they are rightfully named, have some explaining to do.

More than 100 years ago, entomologist Charles Marlatt discovered that cicada larvae aestivate—or lie dormant—in 13- and 17-year periods before tunneling up to breed. Today, biologists recognize more than 30 broods of periodic cicadas and know that each year, at least some of these bugs emerge to sing, mate, and die.

The last big cicada extravaganza is today only a distant, chitinous memory. In my garden, I can find little evidence of the invasion that had me picking and flicking bugs off almost every surface. Apart from an occasional flaky hull on the underside of the picnic table, you'd think they never came at all.

While yet another wave of cicadas dubbed Brood XIV was supposed to visit the northeast again in 2008 (it didn't), scientists are still trying to explain why Brood X of 2004 was not as big a deal as anticipated. They're looking at a number of possible causes, including chemical pollution, property and landscape development, and even a shift in the bugs' natural aestivation cycles. Entomologists report that such "accelerations" may be changing the frequency of cicada emergences in the Mid-Atlantic region.

Still, as we crunched thousands of them underfoot, swept them into piles, cursed their buzzing and—as some brave souls vowed to do—battered, deep fried and munched them, many people cringed at the potential destruction wrought by these bejeweled critters. You could almost see Charlton Heston waving in a plague of locusts.

Here's the thing: As much as gardeners and arborists fretted about the return of these creatures last year, we may have reason to bless them now.

Like earthworms, sand crabs, some bees and other soil-dwellers, periodic cicadas may actually bring a subsequent bounty of horticultural benefits. In fact, the luxuriant shrub and tree growth witnessed in some areas might just be a natural dividend from the return of the cicadas.

Think of it: These sex-starved kazoos bored up half-inch diameter holes from three feet down. What better soil irrigation and aeration device could nature have devised? Depending on where you live, your garden may be burgeoning thanks to the slow, patient work of the very bug many of us dread.

We gladly pay a premium to landscaping companies for aeration, irrigation and fertilization services, right? These bugs excavate *gratis*, both on their way up and on their progeny's way back down into the loam. Cicadas stink, yes, but they industriously till and fertilize your shrubbery beds and trees' root systems.

How sound is this theory? How does the cicada lifecycle ultimately benefit your lawn and backyard flora?

Dr. Michael J. Raupp, cicada expert at University of Maryland College Park, said there's some evidence that the nitrogen released from all of those rotting carcasses may act as a "nutrient pulse" to the plants. "This could be part of the abundant flowering and foliage production," he said.

At the University of California at Davis, Louie H. Yang tested the idea that dead cicadas fertilize the soil and improve tree and shrub growth. After sowing dead cicadas in forests, Yang discovered the soil contained more microbes and two and a half to three times the nutrients of untreated areas. Yang's research, published in *Science* in November 2004, indicates that "resource pulses" of cicadas create "bottom-up cascades" that indirectly affect growth and reproduction in plants.

Government studies on the effects of cicada emergences on the clutch sizes of wild turkeys found that in brood years, the number of poults or hatchlings increases. And research has shown that tree growth rings are wider immediately after brood cycles, suggesting an indirect, salutary effect on root health.

They may have had a beneficial effect on people, too.

"The 2004 emergence made a lot of people aware of insects in a positive way," said Dan Gilrein, extension entomologist for Cornell University Cooperative Extension of Suffolk County. "Excitement and energy surrounded this event—and some frustration and apprehension, as well. But if the emergence of Brood X brought people to entomology in a positive way, that's a wonderful phenomenon."

If the experts are correct, my theory about cicadas-as-gardeners'-assistants will get its next test as early as this year. Invariably, tree branch tips will fall, much to the chagrin of orchard growers. But my point is that, rather than dread their coming, we should welcome the return of the loud bugs with the goo-goo eyes.

They just might be coming back to help. We don't have long to wait.

The Spiders of Autumn

September is spider month at my house.

By that, I don't mean that I feature them on the menu or charge neighborhood kids admission to see them perform in a Spider Circus in the backyard. But September with its balmy, drying winds and slanting Faulknerian light brings out the eight-legged visitors—in droves. They somehow realize, all at about the same time, that vacation's over and that I am beginning the slow process of battening down the house for winter.

"It's just like *Charlotte's Web*," my wife says cheerfully, as a lobster-sized specimen spins in a window just outside the dining room. This one works fast, shrink-wrapping a stricken moth as efficiently as our grocery store butcher.

What, I wonder, do they make of me—a huge blob of infrared heat huffing great clouds of CO_2? They no more want to net me than a fisherman wants to hook a whale. *What would we do with all that meat?* I can hear them thinking.

Scientists say spider venom is ten times more potent in the fall than in spring, attesting possibly to the rush order that nature puts on the waning mild weather. To me, it's a kind of arachnid version of "What are you saving the Chivas for?" Maybe the biggest, tastiest prey need a shot of the good stuff.

Their variety is astounding. There are big black ones, medium orange ones, little grey ones, and tiny brown ones. There are spiders that seem to love the bathroom and spiders that are exclusively basement dwellers. Some inhabit the corners of our bedroom cathedral ceiling, knowing that no power on earth can reach them without a sixteen-foot ladder.

They seem to want to eat everything else that crawls or flies, which is fine with me: moths, mosquitoes, fleas, ants, centipedes, water bugs, wasps, pill bugs, ticks, and other spiders. They are very democratic in their tastes, but unfortunately, I do not think they vote.

Maybe the 10,000 spiders that descend on my house each fall are nature's way of clearing up the detritus of the humid, prodigal summer, when insects by the millions have bred their little brains out on my turf. The sucked-dry husks of bugs I find all over the place tell me that nature runs a pretty tight ship; spiders are the recycling sanitation workers of the insect world.

How autumn spiders enter the house is a mystery. Maybe they hitchhike on our trousers or ball up in the bottom of grocery bags or flatten themselves out under the storm window sashes. However they arrive, they are faithful in their coming, exterminators be damned.

Nobody likes walking into a spider's web, probably because our reptile brains whisper: "It's *on* you." But consider the fate of the poor victim of one urban legend that tells of a woman bitten on the face by a spider. Some days later, she developed a big red bump, which she somehow chose to ignore *at her peril*. A few days later, while brushing her hair, the bristles nicked the red bump open. Thousands, *thousands*, of tiny baby spiders came running out all over her head, face and neck. The story does not tell to which insane asylum the woman was committed or how much tranquilizer they had to pump into her to stop the screaming.

Spiders, next to bats and snakes, are probably most people's least favorite animal. The standard reaction is invariably the same: "Daddy, come kill it!"

But when the spiders descend on my house in the autumn of the year, I tend to do little but get their guest room ready. While other people will gird themselves for a month of killing bugs, I wax philosophical. I've almost come to believe that the spiders realize my house is safe haven. If I ever accidentally reduce myself like the guy in the 1957 sci-fi classic *The Incredible Shrinking Man*, I imagine finding myself among friends, or at least acquaintances. Or, if I somehow ever got jazzed up with radioactive spidey juice like Spiderman Peter Parker, I'd like to think I'd still be a sympathetic landlord.

The Great-Ideas-That-Never-Got-Off-The-Ground Catalogue

Welcome to our Spring Catalogue!

The R&D folks here at New Millennium Products, Inc. have been working overtime to bring you an array of new products this season to make your life easier —or, at least a little more bearable. Because of actions pending in Federal and some state courts, we've discontinued the New Millennium Catalogue Sweepstakes—but that doesn't mean you have to miss out on the savings! Check out these specials:

Rainforest Lumber Patio Set

Made sense about eight and a half years ago when our buyer picked up a steal on an old Liberian freighter abandoned at anchor off Curacao. Oops! How'd we know the Amazon would start disappearing at 500,000 acres a year? Anywho, this sturdy, weatherproof, Mediterranean-style patio ensemble includes missionary table, four captain's chairs, and something that looks like a chaise lounge—but it might just be the pallet the whole thing came on, we're not sure! Earth tone and tan. Some assembly required; hardware not included—sorry! $89.99.

Home Acupuncture Kit

Get rid of those troublesome aches and pains the easy way with our very own Home Acupuncture Clinic.™ Not just a WWII surplus Swedish Army sewing kit, this handy leatherette pouch comes complete with all the pins, needles, multi-colored threads buttons, and patches to soothe most any pain you can name. Includes a rice paper acupuncture body map we found as wrapping on a shipment of imported fruit jar glassware and directions in English we downloaded from an Internet site in Singapore. We're throwing in a special Norwegian Navy fishhook remover (We don't know what you'll use that for, but the label claims "dözens in usages!") Autoclave sterilization to 300° required before use. Non-narcotic and hypoallergenic. Specify pouch in red or tan. $14.99

Mood Band-Aids™

Liquid crystal-impregnated adhesive strips read your aura color, then change to reflect your emotional state. Angry? Mood Band-Aids turn fiery red. Sullen? The Mood Band-Aid blushes cobalt blue. Feeling anxious about that presentation at the office? The Mood Band-Aid goes pale yellow. Perfect gift for your boss, co-workers, ex-spouse, grown children, neighbor or anyone else you need to emotionally "read" in a flash. Not intended for home diagnosis and treatment of psychiatric disorders. Box of twenty strips. $9.99.

The Travel Mojo Bag®

We call it "haunt couture." You'll say it's spooky the way this specially designed sack is roomy enough to carry all of your hoo-doo. It's made out of calf or goatskin, but we could be wrong! It's waterproof inside and out for that "dead head" on your list who has everything. Comes complete with a braided halyard of some kind of weird monkey hair with a hammered brass turnbuckle. There's even a secret pocket in the lining for all those moldy animal fetishes! Will not show up on airport x-ray machines or in mirrors. Specify right or left handed when ordering. Monogramming not available. Blue-black, midnight, peat brown, and wolf's hair. $24.99.

Feng Sui Disco Ball

Does your family room just feel all wrong? Need something to set the balance of forces in your master bedroom? Our 500-facet commercial-grade Feng Sui Disco Ball may just be the answer. This 15-inch diameter "orb of joy" attaches to any overhead light in minutes. Flip the switch and the energy and the whole atmosphere of your house changes in seconds! May not be suitable for nighttime use under some local zoning codes. If the neighbors complain, just tell the police you're working the kinks out of a new alarm system! Step-down transformer for the laser not included. $29.99.

Dashboard Television™

Never miss an episode of your favorite program again with the television for people on the go. This solid-state dashboard TV installs easily into the speedometer casing of most American model SUVs and light trucks. Features a six-inch color screen with full stereo sound. It's crush-proof and will stand up to the worst the highway has to dish out. And speaking of dish, for just an additional $19.95, you'll get a fully articulating eighteen-inch satellite dish for your SUV or truck roof to pull in those hard to get access channels! Comes with 64-pin wiring harness and 300-page color manual. Some installation required. Not street legal in the District of Columbia, Virgin Islands, or Puerto Rico. $199.99.

Nicotyme™ Quiet Hour™ Flow-Through™ teabags

Need a late afternoon pick-me-up but no time for a cigarette break? Got a 4:00 p.m. meeting and just can't wait for a nicotine fix? This is just the solution—and so tasty, too! Just place one bag in a cup, add boiling water and presto—the perfect rush before rush hour. Goes well as garnish in a dry martini. Avoid operating machinery or attempting to sleep after use. May cause irritability in children. May NOT be rolled and smoked. Box of 60 bags. $8.99 plus applicable state sales tax.

The When™ Bracelet

A great gift idea for the holidays! It's an indicator bracelet that tells you and others when you've had enough to drink. When™ works on the same principle as our popular Mood Band-Aid™ by chemically sensing on your skin the by products of alcohol being metabolized in your liver! The When™

bracelet starts out clear and gets increasingly cloudy as you consume more alcohol. When it's completely opaque, you're done! No more arguing about how much you've had to drink—and if you don't like it, let's just step outside and settle this, pal! Endorsed by police in three Florida counties. Must be 21 years old to order. Comes with a full, lifetime guarantee and a note to your wife. Set of three; just like handcuffs, one size fits all! $15.99.

Thank You in Advance

Dear Valued Customer:

We are writing to tell you how much we value your business and to thank you in advance for your continued patronage.

Many of our customers have written to comment on our policy of ending our correspondence with the phrase, "Thank you in advance."

In fact, quite a number of you explained that you did not understand the point of our thanking you for something you had not done yet.

To answer these concerns about our policy of thanking you in advance, we asked our marketing and public relations specialists to answer some of your most "frequently asked questions."

Thank you in advance for carefully considering our corporate rationale for thanking you in advance. Please don't hesitate to contact us with any further concerns.

—The Customer Service Department

Q: *Why "thank you in advance?" Isn't that a little presumptuous?*

A: Not at all. The social and commercial history of the use of the phrase "thank you in advance" roughly coincides with the rise in the widespread use of consumer credit in the United States throughout the 1950s and 60s. As consumers became accustomed to charging their purchases on credit, they gradually demanded a more sophisticated level of customer service etiquette. Hence, the traditional "thank you" evolved quite naturally into "thank you in advance." Customers have come to perceive added value in our expressing our gratitude *ahead of time.*

Q: *That sounds like a load of unvarnished bunkum.*

A: Thank you in advance for your question.

Q: *Has your company secretly mastered some form of time travel? I mean, can your customer service representatives shuttle things like my credit card payments, my dry cleaning, and my cell phone battery back and forth in the time-space continuum and cause things to happen in the future? If that's the case, couldn't you be running the risk of creating one of those crazy ' it's-already-happened-in-the-future' loops, like in the* Terminator *movies?*

A: While our company has always prided itself on being on the cutting edge of consumer technology, we know of no way to make things happen in the future. That would be a physical impossibility—or so the people in our shipping department tell us.

Q: *So how come people in the movies travel back from the future with no clothes on?*
A: Simple. Nyrflon hasn't been invented yet.

Q: *When you thank me in advance, it makes me feel as if I have no options. What about free will?*

A: Certainly you have free will. If he were alive today, Kant might point out that you can choose between 17 different colors of fleece pullovers in nine different sizes from our spring catalogue, for example. If everything were set and unchangeable, your entire life would have been determined before you were born. It'd be like singing with the Jackson Five or playing for the New York Mets.

Q: *Thanking me in advance sounds just like my neighbor Leon, who works nights as a warehouse foreman, but whom everybody suspects is really a gangster running a freight-tampering scheme. He gives us boxes of cheap crockery and wineglasses and says:" You'll like this stuff." I feel vaguely intimidated.*

A: You got a question somewhere in that?

Q: *Are you at all connected, is what I'm asking, in any way with the mob? I mean, "Thank you in advance" could be interpreted as "How'd you like a limp for life?"*

A: What are you, a comedian?

Q: *As a teacher, I am constantly telling my students that adding extra words to their writing is wasteful of the reader's time. I tell them that E.B. White's advice about writing with precision and elegance is wise. Am I wrong?*

A: Certainly, notwithstanding.

Q: *What?*

A: Sometimes gratuitous verbiage makes you feel better, right? "Gesundheit," for example. Or "Have a nice day." Or "You get two sides with that."

Q: *So then, are you just pushy– or what? "Thank you in advance" sounds like you're trying to twist my arm. Use undue influence. Light a fire under me. Kill me with kindness. Why for God's sake can't you just say "Thank you"?*

A: Don't make us come over there.

"I'm TCT 1000. I'll be your server this evening."

Gaia

Dead of winter?
—in winter you hear it best:
ground breathing beneath your feet,
supplely creaking and moving.

Just beneath the surface
the thick tissue of life,
a uterine wall in black loam,
reticulated, patient roots.

They know her as children,
creatures of the moist and dark,
the vole, the grub, the blind termite.
Slowly, they suckle.

Worms know her best.
Empty sides in, they slide in her,
filling and sipping her ripe ooze,
drunk on the fecundity.

If you bury a stone,
she will heave it up;
if you lay down a branch,
she will cover it.

The landscape has no memory.
Fences cant and sag,
even as we walk, feet pressed to her,
pacing off our mortal geographies.

Faces

In the newspaper,
the terrorists
half-lidded, heavy-lipped,
like women ready to make love,
make me wonder about
mothers, sisters, wives, lovers
with the sweetness of kohl on them
like spider's silk
who weave or bake
in the heat and musk
amid music like a lamb's bleat.

Were these men
we can imagine
sharing milkshakes and boardwalk photos,
with peach-colored Florida or Delaware girls
who loved them for a weekend
—because they laughed and talked of flying—
who knew nothing else about them?

When the towers fell,
I remembered
Babel, Goshen, and Sodom
where ground opens
where water flows
from desert rock.

An Arab I know once said:
"I am a man of the desert.
No one laughs at my beard."
The cheek of that,
and of when we are told,
finally, that God is great.

At My First Bar Mitzvah

At my first *bar mitzvah*
I was forty-six
and one impressed Catholic
when his mentors helped Jake
embrace the scroll as big as he was
from which he read in halting tones
the words of his fathers.

When Jake's dad wept,
I heard
"This is my beloved son
in whom I am well pleased."

We all laughed when
the rabbi said not to hit
the guest of honor too hard
as we tossed hard candy at the boy
about whom all sweet hopes
for the future
had been spoken.

September's Child

for Grace

It rained all night
when you were born,
the low drawing you
down in a furious tide,
rushing you into
our shaking arms,
before the doctor
had found a parking place.

We felt an awkward holiness when,
in your purpled crown,
we saw your kinship
with the stars
forecasting not untroubled joy
for those who will not wait
to be born.

Plato's Tree

"Plato's Tree, in whose shade the ancient Greek is said to have taught his philosophy 2,300 years ago, lay uprooted and torn yesterday, the victim of a modern-day traffic accident."

—The Associated Press

The sunshine is almost audible,
as a bus comes up the street
swerves by the roadside
into the tree
which cracks and falls
into four pieces
like a bad argument.
From the shattered trunk rush hundreds of insects.
No one takes note
as the sun fries their soft, white bodies.
They do not know what is going on.

A policeman walks up and scratches
an almond-shaped suck mark on his upper arm,
thinking about Madame Duous in her featherbed in town,
her soft white body like an octopus.
He does not know what is going on.

A tourist points a camera at the scene,
presses the shutter,
and closes his eyes.

Washing an Apple for my Daughter

Home sick at eight
she waits with fevered patience
as I prepare with ceremony
a macintosh, her favorite.

We've colored and beaded and puppet-showed
afternoon-channel-surfed past
people tearing each other's hearts out
before a live studio audience,
to get to something anything,
the news, a cooking show.

My love for her is in the labor that
I know she will not see or taste or smell
until in the ripeness of time
she might bear her own fruit.

Running water,
water over the skin,
I carefully pare an apple down,
down, not knowing how to tell her what's ahead.

Lucifer-like, do I make her world too sweet
as I hand her the fruit,
sure that everything depends on her
her tiny, perfect *thank you?*

Mourning, River, Rocks

Perfect preference is for poems
that don't explain,
since who requires a homily
from the mourning dove
or a preamble by river water over rocks?

If you want my attention,
buy me a beer;
but in telling me you wrote
something after a walk
through a soft rain with
a madwoman you are seeing
but don't love, you make me
wonder if it's the poem
or the woman that worries you.

And if it's the woman, introduce me,
and buy her a beer, too.

Otherwise, put that one aside,
and tell me what the dove says
about mourning, river, rocks.

The Red Wheelbarrow

with apologies to WCW

so what depends

upon

a red wheel

barrow

filling with rain

water

beside some wet

chickens?

Ice Maker

The icemaker in my freezer
knows the nature of counterpoint,
of slow continents and ocean forces.

At night it clicks and cracks
like glacial drift, tectonic plates,
knocking icy bones

In a crystalline eureka:
the icemaker *warms up* for a moment,
a quick, hot instant

Like a Chinese finger prison
only calm, inward pressure
relaxes the wicker, releases fingers.

Or the way love
demands negation of *I*,
or the nautilus spirals out of its own cuticle.

In the dark middle of the freezer,
paradox plays out,
retrograde of opposites

—not magic—but brief reversal
of the water's fortune,
which felt itself frozen forever

before knocking, wet and glassy,
like cold atoms in the bones of the sea,
shocked into essence by the slow and silent maker.

Ignis Fatuus

My grandfather was an electrician,
the old vacuum-tube, screw-in-fuse, knob-and-tube kind,
who dreamed in amperes, watts, and volts,
who called light bulbs *globes,*
and offered strange advice:

When a globe burns out, slowly and gently twist one third turn,
reigniting the filament to extend the life.

Clean dust from cold globes with a damp cloth since
the deficit of dirt is a shortened life.

Never handle a globe by the glass where oils from your fingers
heat it unevenly and shorten the life.

Don't screw a globe tight, since the hot metal base expands,
cracks the receptacle, and shortens the life.

Turning globes on-off
shortens the life.

The filament burns brightest
just before the end.

Then no
slow and gentle hands
damp cloth
oils
loosening fingers
can reignite the filament

in the cold turning globes.

Suite:
This Plastic Art

I.

Connelly drives the countryside, seeking quarry.

He stalks an oak branch,

on a moss bed near a brook.

He locks it in the trunk.

Pinned between two cinderblocks in the studio,

it bites his fingers, blunts his chisel.

He tortures wings as they emerge,

rasps and sands the head into twisted upsweep.

This albatross is adamant.

Impaled on a shaft of steel, it hovers over granite

and would unperch to find forest again

if he hadn't dipped its soul in the sea.

He writes "NFS" on the tag

and smokes another cigarette.

II.

In Florence, the docents are mute.

Bars on the windows of the Michelangelo Museum

obscure the view of the Arno.

Inside sit versions of the Unfinished Pieta,

statues he carved at eighty.

Mary is fat and has Chianti-jug biceps;

Jesus is a mass of writhing marble,

the face a mask of chisel marks.

Feeling his waning hammer,

did he try to destroy it,

as his students pulled him away?

It is hard to believe, after closing time,

these gorgons do not wrestle.

III.

Connelly rails.

"This plastic art asks hard questions:

'Can you freeze in frieze?'

'Is suffering relieved in bas-relief?'"

The fragments give him cold reply.

"Damn it, that is *not* all we need to know, John Keats.

For tell us

how—in the hands of Rodin

plying the clay of a Thinker's calf—

we might not see Christ's wet fingers

wrapped on the cross?"

He lights another cigarette

and begins again.

Suicides in Heaven

Sunday morning with the newspaper

browsing sports pages and doing puzzles,

brings an item about a woman who

threw herself off the quay

where the Jones Falls empties into the Chesapeake.

She spoke to a passerby

who remembered a flowered yellow dress.

I wondered

what suicides do in heaven

what it must be like to show up there

suddenly.

And I imagine suicides in heaven are mute.

They stand in the back

having nothing to add.

Having no bodies

no one knows they are present

which is the true hell of it

Even on Sunday mornings when

reading the paper

someone sees something remarkable.

She shifts her weight from foot to foot,

the way she did on the quay

that autumn afternoon as

the water taxies shuttled back and forth

and the suds came down the Falls in clumps

past the feet of dawdling school children,

like clouds.

Dead or Missing

I know a lady in Munich
almost ninety and waiting,
has withered from waiting.
She makes obscure remarks, like,
"Someone is always crazy;
when two are, it's worse."
That is the logic of two world wars and
fifty million suburban Munich parlors
with gray photographs telling stories
the newspaper lists never could.

Hers was a handsome young *Korporal*,
another for the Eastern Front,
which told any simple visitor who wondered,
the difference between *Gefallen* and *Vermisst*.
For seventy years, since the September morning
he boarded the train and stormed away,
there has been silence.
Russia is that wide.

She dreams of a day when her granddaughter
comes, rapping, *Oma, wir haben Post*—
"Grandmother, the mailman is here."

Destiny at Knifepoint

"Poets have been mysteriously silent on the subject of cheese."

—G.K. Chesterton

(1874-1936)

For one thing, the funny names,
Feta, Munster, Brie,
fare better on the plate.

Some we pronounce together,
like names of grandparents:
Gouda and Edam.

It's all the same.
Milk with a rind.
Cream with attitude.

But it lives and breathes,
like wine, like people,
aroma beyond aroma.

It is not indescribable:
mown meadow at dawn,
a salty cellar wall, cow's must.

Who can forget a bolus of Stilton on the tongue?
Grounded, an essence—it's not the ocean—
The place we came from, where we go.

"You growl, girl."

The Fabulist

Hal

How did I get talked into taking a three-day trek into the mountains of Pennsylvania in the middle of winter with my ex-girlfriend and her *other* ex-boyfriend? My life seemed already complicated enough and I was still nursing a humongous thing for Trish, our mutual love interest. But it wasn't so hard when the other ex, Devon Carpenter, explained that we were walking up a long trail to his dying grandfather's house for what might be his final visit.

It was then I decided I could be a hero and accomplish a long-standing family mission that I knew would make my parents happy. Agnostics at heart, we still had the box in the closet at my parents' house that contained the ashes of my own paternal grandfather. He had been a life-long farmer and his last wish was that his ashes get scattered somewhere in the Pennsylvania countryside. What better place than two thousand feet up the southern face of Turner's Switch?

In addition to having been one of my rivals for the affections of Tricia Baker, Devon was both my team captain and chief nemesis on the St. Ignatius University cross country team for those past three years. I still remember chasing the white kerchief she had tied around Devon's bicep just before he tore out in front of us in our last home meet against Salisbury and Hopkins. Through my salt-burning eyes, I watched the kerchief bob up and down, like the tail of some mythical stag I had to catch.

Now I am up in the clouds with friends who play games like enemies, and I guess I am willing to be a player one last time, too. We've made a pact to keep our cell phones turned off for the duration of the trip up the mountain, which I know is a real sacrifice for Trish, who's one of the hottest mamacitas in our class. There are new boytoys on her shelf all the time, it seems.

Does Trish still have a thing for me? I don't know. Do I have something to prove to Devon? Probably. And I know I have something to prove to myself.

Trish

His grandfather will tell us three stories, Devon says again, squaring his backpack on his shoulders as we follow him up the mountain.

It's a hard climb, it's snowing now, and the trail is steep and slick. Devon hikes ahead of us. I'm falling behind. My breath is coming short and heavy, billowing from my mouth and nose in frosty clouds. Hal lags back for me. Which is part of my plan. He is steaming from beneath his parka. I cannot tell if I am steaming. Devon, whose head is enveloped in vapor, is almost out of sight above us. Hal moves alongside me.

"How did he get this house up here anyway?" I ask Hal. I think about teasing him into turning back, of descending to the car and level ground, to a warm fire and maybe his hands on me. That would really set Devon off.

"That must be one of the three stories," Hal says. We both sit back on a large boulder, laying our skis on its green-grey hump. Hal hands me one of a couple clementines he says he's been saving. We eat the juicy cold wedges and look down the mountain in the direction we've come.

We've traded a half dozen miles from the car, fifteen miles from the highway, forty from Breezewood, and a morning's drive from the city for this weekend visit to Devon's grandfather's house atop a Pennsylvania mountain in the snow.

"There must be a surfaced road on the other side of the mountain," Hal says. "Leave it to Devon to deliberately ignore a road for miles of this."

"I'm dying," I tell him. My arms are limp at my sides. Hal's face is bright red against the short blonde hair sticking from his ski cap. There is no mistaking him for a mountaineer; he looks like a little boy with rosy cheeks.

I resent Devon for luring us up here, but I'm curious about him and this grandfather. And the three stories. Devon seems at once anxious and unable to explain them.

I give Hal my biggest, winky-face smile. "Wanna' carry my skis, lover?"

Hal gives me his *Don't give me that* look. "I thought you were taking ballet this semester."

I know Hal doesn't trust me anymore and there's nothing I can do to get back to that place we were a year ago. It's so annoying.

"Aerobics, not ballet, and they don't teach you to scale mountains. We're pretty high up, aren't we, Hal?"

"Way up." He points to a range of mountains to the north. "Scranton is that way."

Hal looks off through the snowy trees. I follow the line of his chin to his brow. There's crystallized water vapor in his hair, and while I am looking at it, I keep getting the feeling that what I am feeling is love for this boy. His nostrils flare. He sighs heavily, yawns.

I know it's, like, really over between us, but want to touch him, have him touch me, even through our heavy clothes and gloves.

"Here," he says, taking my skis from the boulder, "I'll be your skis-bitch just this once. Bunjee them on my backpack with mine."

Devon's voice yodels down on us from farther up the trail. "Boys and girls!" His voice echoes down and resounds in the valley.

Hal and I look at each other, amazed, when we reach Devon. He has made a fire, has begun to cook.

"What a surprise," I say, unceremoniously dropping my pack to the ground.

"Devon, why don't we push on and eat at the house?" Hal says. "It can't be much farther."

I look down at my pack. "Come to think of it, it would be warmer."

Devon

I am working with the fire and the utensils. I don't look up. "I'm hungry," I tell them.

Trish and Hal exchange glances as they sit down on broad stones I've heated by the fire.

I'm making a venison stew for dinner with frozen meat I've packed along. They warm their feet and hands by the fire and watch my fingers cut and section the dark red meat with my big hunting knife.

"Aren't there any deer this high up?" Trish asks.

I wipe the flat blade on my jeans and in a quick motion push it into the sheath strapped to my calf.

"The deer are down in the valley," I tell her. "There are a few more houses down there. There're salt licks in the creeks and in some yards."

"Devon, you sound like a bio major," Hal says. He and Trish are history majors. I am an econ major with a marketing minor.

Hal's still pissed that I started seeing Trish after him. And about my winning the MVP for the season last fall.

I know Trish is still excited to see me, but she's playing it really, really cool.

So I reach over to my pack and pull out my pistol.

Hal

In another quick movement, Devon has a revolver from his knapsack.

"But if I did see a deer I'd drop it like a dog with this," he says.

I feel the hair on my neck crawl. Trish gasps his name.

"You always carry that thing?" I try not to let him know this is another surprise, another piece for the puzzle.

"Usually, when I'm alone," he says. "There're always packs of wild dogs up here. Like wolves, only they're not much bigger than pit bulls."

As we eat the stew Devon has made, he tells us a story about killing wild dogs in the middle of the night without a flashlight.

"Their eyes, they gleam in the starlight. Like raccoons."

I see Trish look around at the darkening trees and shiver.

"When my grandfather and his brother built the house up here, there were still mountain lions."

"There were *what?*" Trish drops her spork on her plate.

"Cougars. Mountain lions. You know—panthers."

"Devon, are you kidding?" she laughs.

"No. It was just like in the movies. There were bears and bobcats, too. There's one up at the house, stuffed. It's kinda' like that Hemingway story, the one about the big mountain in Africa—"

"Kilimanjaro," I say.

"That's it," He says. "Like the part where it says near the peak of the mountain is the dried up carcass of a leopard, and how nobody knows what the leopard was looking for up there in the snow."

"I always wondered about that," I say, teasing him. "I always thought that the epigraph should have read, 'No one has explained what *the men* were seeking at that altitude.'"

Devon looks thoughtful for a minute.

"But then the whole thing wouldn't have made any sense."

"I don't know, Devon. Just forget it."

"Do you have a license for that thing?" Trish asks.

"Nope. Built it from a kit."

We watch the fire. It is growing dark around us.

Trish

Suddenly, Devon points the gun in the air, straight up, and shoots the gun. I hear myself let out a shriek. This is another one of the reasons I broke it off with Devon: he's completely unpredictable.

"Devon!" Hal jumps up and starts talking fast now. "It's going to come right down on us at terminal velocity, you idiot."

Devon leers at us. "Relax. You sound like a physics major."

"Put the gun away, Devon," I say. "You're being stupid. You're so fuck-ing irresponsible."

He shrugs and crazily mouths the syllables of "What-Ev-Er" and buries the pistol in his pack.

"Just letting him know we're here, he says. "That's all I was doing."

"You might have killed one of us," Hal says. "Once they go up, they have to come down."

"It blew away," Devon says, kicking his feet into the fire, knocking it apart.

"Look at the sparks, man," Hal says. "They're going straight up. There's no wind tonight."

A cloud of cinders from the fire shimmers into the trees.

"Let it go. You're alive, aren't you?" Devon says. "Plenty of people fire guns everyday and never get scratched."

He stands up, pulls on his pack, and tramps the fire into the slush that's formed around it.

"Don't worry about cleaning that pot now. Just carry it up to the house, will you?" he tells us.

He is off into the darkness above us before we can get up.

"Follow the trail and bear right at the fork. The house is on the right side. Can't miss it," he says from the darkness.

Hal

We finish breaking the camp, tamping out the fire.

"You were hating on him pretty hard there," I say as we start up the hill after Devon.

"I don't know. He's always goading me about his being a nihilist, that the one thing he believes in the hardest is nothing," she says. "And yet he's always the one ragging on people because of their random hook-ups and their 'whatever' attitudes. I guess that was just a flashback to old words we've had." She looks at me closely. "You don't believe everything's a big Nothing."

"I haven't decided yet," I tell her. "I make up my mind one day that existence is rich with beaucoup meaning, and then I hear something that really makes me wonder." I knew Trish loved these existential departures. And I had a couple of new ones for her.

"Like what?"

"Well, for example the story about the man who was killed by a Federal musket ball over a hundred years after it was fired during the Civil War. The bullet lodged in a tree trunk. They cut the tree down decades and decades later. The man works in a sawmill, and the blade of the saw strikes the slug with such force at just the right angle to deflect it out of the log and into the worker," I tell her. "I am impressed by several things in that story. One of them is that the bullet may have killed twice: once during the war, once in the saw mill."

"But it was just an accident," she says.

"Remember, I said 'just the right angle' to kill the man. Doesn't it strike you that the '*right* angle' for the story is precisely the *wrong* angle for the mill worker?"

"First of all, I don't believe it ever happened. Cite your sources." Trish says.

"I read about that on the Ripley's Believe It Or Not website. Supposedly, if you go to the Ripley's Museum, they have to show your evidence of that event."

"Oh—*really* great source," she says laughing.

"I imagine that would be a pretty interesting job for an historian," I say, as I help her with her pack.

"What, trying to prove that whacked out, random, events actually have some existential meaning?"

"No. Working at the Ripley Museum," I say, as we start up the trail towards the summit. "And here's another amazing fact for you: I've got *my* grandfather in my backpack here."

Trish stops, grabs my arm, and looks at me, startled.

"You *what?*"

"In a box. It's perfectly safe. It's a sealed container. I brought him up here to scatter his ashes. It was his last request."

"Oh, my God. That's so—*cool!* How—when are you going to do it?"

"I thought later tonight. I figure I can do it after everybody's in bed. Supposed to be a full moon. Want to help me?"

I can see Trish is fascinated, and she nods.

"I am so there," she says.

"Devon says on the front side of the house is a scenic overlook. Panoramic view of the valley right down to the bottom of Turner's Switch," I say. "I figure in the moonlight we can pour my granddad's ashes off and watch them sprinkle down into the valley amid the falling snow. Then when the rains come in the spring, they'll wash him down the Switch into the bottom country. That's where he wanted to end up."

Trish stares at me and smiles.

"That's one of the most beautiful things I've ever heard," she says. She leans into me and gives me one of her patented wet kisses on my cheek. My mission is close to being accomplished, I tell myself.

Devon

My grandfather's house is a huge log lodge with granite foundations. There are lights on in several rooms and several cars parked in the gravel drive that winds around to the other side of the house. I wonder whose they are. I drop my pack on the porch and go in and up the long staircase.

When Trish and Hal reach the top of the trail, I go out to greet them at the doorstep in my shirtsleeves. I show them into the cavernous living room where somebody has built a fire in the great stone fireplace.

I must have a funny look on my face or something.

"Devon, what's wrong?" Trish asks me, sensing something before Hal does.

"He's sick," I tell them. "The doctor's up there right now. There might not be any stories tonight. I'll get us something to drink."

The room is half-lit by the fire. A huge buck's head stares down from one wall above my grandfather's gun case. The whole house smells of wood smoke, leather, and the oak logs that form the walls of the place.

Trish sits in one of the big wingback chairs as I come back with a handle of bourbon and three glasses.

"Sorry, Trish. There's no vodka. But I think there's ginger ale in the kitchen if you want to mix," I tell her.

I pour three shots and hand the glasses out. "My uncle Jack from Philly and the doctor are upstairs with him now. He's been bedridden for the past couple of days," I say. "We're trying to reach my Dad in Seattle but apparently he's got no service or something."

I walk to the fire and throw back the whiskey.

"I was hoping we'd get to hear a story tonight," I say. That's the way he always did it, at night by the fire. One a night."

Hal sits in one of the big comfortable chairs. My grandfather's massive meerschaum pipe that has long bled into hues of amber is at his elbow.

Hal sips his drink dainty like a woman. I think maybe he's going gay on me or something.

"Who takes care of him?" Hal asks.

I pour myself another and hold the handle up in the air, shaking it between them. Both Trish and Hal toss theirs back and I pour again.

"My uncle was getting up here about once a week," I tell them. "Recently there's been a nurse every couple of days. Then there's the cook. She's only woman who's lived with him since my grandmother died, right after I was born. So that's—let's see, more than, like, twenty years." I toss my second shot. "But he's not feeling real swift. I don't think we'll get a story tonight."

Trish stretches her wet stocking feet near the fire. "You tell us about the three stories," she says.

I kick at the fire. I've got a funny feeling or something in the bottom of my stomach.

Trish

Devon stands by the big hearth.

"The way he used to do it was that each night he'd tell a different story. Each story was different," he says. "One was a kind of kids' story, a fable. It was about two seeds that sit around in the ground and talk about a lot of things, like what they want to be when they grow up. I really can't remember it too well. I think one seed became a tree. The other seed became a tree that made the handle of the hatchet that chopped the other tree down. I don't know, though."

He studies the fire. We finish our shots.

"Then on the second night he'd tell the second story. It was like a story for older kids," Devon says. "That's how it went. The first was a baby's story, the second was a teenager's story, and the third one was a grown-up's story. The teenager's story was about an Indian kid who had to prove his manhood by counting coup on another kid his age from another tribe. Counting coup was like playing tag with tomahawks. Any way, this one kid didn't have the courage to do it, so he couldn't get a feather and stuff. He wandered around in the woods until something happened to him, but I can't exactly remember what. I think…he fell off a cliff saving a little kid and turned into a bird or something."

Devon looks towards the stairs as an older man comes down.

"Devon, would you come here for a moment?" the man says.

Devon walks halfway across the room.

"Would you come upstairs? We're going to have to make some phone calls."

"Uncle Jack, I was telling my friends about the three stories."

"Come up, Devon."

Devon looks back at us. Is he frightened? I want to hug him, but he turns and quickly walks up the stairs after his uncle.

Hal

Trish begins to cry quietly.

I wonder if we should now even try to scatter my granddad's ashes tonight. I was thinking Trish and I would get a little closer.

Devon comes back when the fire has burned low.

"I wanted him to tell the three stories," he repeats. "I wanted to come up here and hear the three stories one last time. I don't think I can remember them all myself. Uncle Jack can't…"

"I'm sorry, Devon," Trish and I say, almost in unison.

"There was the one about the two seeds, one about the Indian bird boy and—I can't remember the third one at all. He'd tell it on the third night. In winter, we'd roast chestnuts and walnuts he'd collected all fall. They were good. Sometimes I'd get to sip beer…"

Devon walks out of the living room, distracted. Trish and I sit and stare at the embers of the fire. Her face is beautiful in the cinnamon and orange light.

We both jump when we hear the shots. Uncle Jack bolts down the stairs and we meet him at the front door. We race outside to the driveway, to the sound of the shots.

We see him, unclearly at first, then fully bathed in the moonlight, as our eyes adjust.

He is standing in the driveway, looking up, holding the gun above his head, firing straight into the air. Trish is sobbing near me and I put my arm around her. Uncle Jack dashes for the gun when it begins clicking. He is a powerfully built man, and he binds Devon's arms to his sides, gently. Devon seems to deflate. He is weeping.

His uncle moves him into the shelter of the big granite portico.

The sky is clear, cloudless. There is no wind tonight.

I do not move or even dare to breathe as I wait for the bullets to stall, to burn in a moment of fixed ascent, and fall back.

The Prophet

At first, Suzanne figured the sounds her husband Buster said he heard were just the residue of some weird dreams. When she noticed they had begun to seep into his waking thoughts, she looked it up in the big family health encyclopedia she kept under her side of the bed. It was getting dog-eared after three kids' worth of sore throats and earaches, and the spine had started to split in the middle of the chapter on menopause.

"Says here that 'prednisone, diet pills, and certain antihistamines can in-duce hallucinations and delusions,'" she read to him one Saturday afternoon, "'including visual, auditory, and olfactory characteristics.'"

They were sitting on the side porch reading and listening to their twin fifteen-year-olds, Mallory and Edward, play basketball out in the driveway.

The afternoon light slanted across the porch railings, settling in long golden rivulets on the porch tiles, where the unusually warm early autumn air held the mingled aromas of charcoal lighter from the grill and mown grass from the back yard.

"Ever see or smell anything funny?"

She watched him look up at her over his drugstore reading glasses, purse his lips, and shake his head slowly. He was reading the part of the Sunday paper that always came on Saturday. She knew that Buster thought these sec-tions were about the things in life that really mattered and therefore had no hard news value: Travel, Real Estate, Food, Home and Garden.

"You haven't taken prednisone since you had that bad case of poison ivy back in 1996," she said. "And you don't touch antihistamines because of your blood pressure."

"And as for diet pills, stay tuned," he said, patting his belly through his t-shirt, where a small but voluptuous fender of skin had begun to appear in the past few years. He didn't get much exercise but to play golf a few times a season. That and pushing the mower around their acre lot on weekend afternoons. Like everybody else in their suburb of Baltimore, they lived a life that required their firing not one mitochondria's worth of energy beyond what was absolutely necessary. They all barbequed and sailed and every so often one of the neighbors' kids would roll an SUV on the way to a Ravens' game with hip hop blaring on the eight-speaker sound system, spare change, CDs, and empties falling all around them.

She was thankful that Clarissa, their oldest daughter, had never texted them with that news. She had graduated with honors from one of the private schools in north Baltimore and had gone off to college flush with success that August.

"I'm sure she does all the same things we did," Buster told Suzanne on the way back from packing her off. "Nothing ever really changes."

Nothing changes? Suzanne's heart beat back against that idea: she believed at least that people had the *potential* to change. Hadn't some kind of parent gene kicked in when they saw their babies sluice wet and wriggling into the world, helped them cope with all the furious, dangerous novelty of raising kids? First successful potty session. First swing set. First tooth. First bicycle. First broken bone. First date. First driving lesson. First day of college. After all, hadn't she and Buster *grown* to become responsible parents? Sure, they still listened to rock and roll, but they also had season subscriptions to the symphony and the opera.

She heard Buster wax philosophic. "Rock is about glorious, unlicensed love," he insisted when she'd go on like that about their past. "Opera is about glorious, dutiful death."

Suzanne thought that maybe Buster's job as a television station cameraman might have had something to do with the things he claimed to be hearing, and ever since the cell-phone-brain-tumor scare, she suspected that microwaves from the big towers up on TV Hill in Hampden might be very gradually cooking all of their nervous systems. She thought Buster might just be getting bigger doses than everyone else.

She reminded him that Jerry Warner, the popular veteran anchorman at Buster's station, had only lived to be sixty-five.

"Jerry Warner smoked like the Marlboro Man," Buster said. "He had two orange fingers on one hand."

She shrugged and went back to the medical book—to a section about hysterical paralysis. Maybe Clarissa's sports medicine course would help sort out what was ailing Buster, but Suzanne wouldn't see her again until Thanksgiving break.

When they had packed Clarissa's trunk for college, Suzanne had added a box of a dozen condoms and a 4-pack of energy-saving florescent light bulbs.

Clarissa paused, then waved her hand over the packages. "What are they for?"

"For those nights when the lights go out," Suzanne said. "Be prepared. Don't drink out of other people's cups. And use the cell phone headset I gave you."

"Mom, cell phones do *not* cause brain cancer," Clarissa said, annoyed at having to tell her mother this again and again. "There are no longitudinal studies to back up that claim."

Suzanne refolded Clarissa's jeans. "And in the 50s and 60s, the tobacco companies tried to convince people menthol cigarettes were good you."

"That never stopped *you* from smoking, mother," she said. "You Baby Boomers are all alike."

When Buster began taking sick days off from work, she started leaving all the windows open at night.

A house has got to breathe. At least that's what her grandfather used to say. He would know, too, because he built two of them, mostly with his and his brother's bare hands. Her father and his brother who were only sixteen and twelve had helped pour the foundations on their parents' house in the early

1930s. She always loved the old place and when her father died and willed her the house, there was never any question where she would live after she got married.

They could go into the basement and see the big red and brown speckled fieldstones embedded like dinosaur bones in the foundation.

Her mother said she thought it charming, but her father said it was really a cheap way to pour a foundation—used less cement that way.

What's wrong with saving a little money here and there when you can, her mother had said. They had built her grandparents' house with a high, post-and-beam frame and mansard roof. The attic had no collar joists and a gable window on each end of the attic for ventilation. The enormous clapboard house stood up on a hillside, overlooking the Jones Falls Valley, surrounded by a suburban development of what Suzanne called "phony-colonies." She kept wearing her tie-dyed blouses and lots of silver bracelets.

The story of Buster's voices and his missing days from work was out around the neighborhood, at the swim club, on the golf course, at the garden club, and Suzanne felt strange to hear that people were talking in undertones about her husband, although she knew that it had been her fault the story had leaked out. Amid those four o'clock glasses of wine with Janet Dugan and Sally McCready, her two next door neighbors, in the slanting light of late August, she had told them about Buster's voices, then couldn't remember having talked about it, like reverse *déja vu*.

The first person to come to see about Buster was Dr. Isherwood, a Johns Hopkins neurologist who lived with his wife and one daughter down the block. He was Buster's age, a skinny guy—a runner—with brown horn-rimmed glasses. He approached Suzanne about the voices at Mallory's field hockey practice one cool evening in early October. All the girls, in honor of Halloween, had fingerpainted designs on their faces in black and orange—not their teams' colors—and howled as they tore around the practice field Indian file with Mallory in the lead. He told her he had heard about Buster's condition at the swim club crabfeast.

"If he keeps presenting these symptoms, tell Buster to give me a call," Isherwood said. "It could be nothing. But the tests we can do today are damn near miraculous."

A week later, Buster did call him and Dr. Isherwood gave Buster a complete neuro work-up that came up completely negative.

Suzanne sat in on the interview Isherwood conducted with Buster that covered just about everything—every possible cause: concussion? (mild, when he was ten or twelve) Family history of tinnitus? migraines? epilepsy? (no, no, and no).

"If you had a metal plate or shrapnel in your skull, I'd almost think you were receiving AM signals through your molars. But your scans and EEG show no abnormalities."

He handed Buster a small box full of blister packs of some blue pills.

"Here's a sample of something we've had some success with. Follow the directions and call me in a week if you're still hearing things."

"And then what?" Suzanne asked.

"I have the name of very good head doctor I can recommend."

"Head doctor?" Suzanne was defensive.

"I'm just saying we can explore all the possibilities."

"I open my mind to the potential burgeoning of the infinite," Buster said. Both Suzanne and Dr. Isherwood looked at him and at each other wide-eyed.

A few days later, some of the other neighbors started showing up to listen to Buster. One afternoon, Suzanne found him out on the side porch, sitting on the big wicker settee, his feet pulled up under him, expounding to Whit Dugan and Jim McCready, the next door neighbors on either side, about why people should hang their clothes in the closet with the hanger hooks pointing outward.

"A thief in the night will find it impossible to steal your clothes," he said. "Their reach will be confounded by the *yang*," Buster told them. "If you point the hooks facing out, they will struggle with the *yang* to take the clothing out."

Both Dugan and McCready slugged their beers and rubbed their chins, nodding at Buster's pronouncements. They thought Buster's suggestion was pretty good, but both wondered what the hell a "yang" was.

As Suzanne carried the bags of groceries into the house, she saw the twins, Mallory and Edward, watching a reality show in the family room. Suzanne could only guess at just what a reality show might be all about.

"Mom, you gotta' get him to talk to someone," Mallory said. "He's out there talking crazy."

Edward sat up. "Worst thing, the neighbors are starting to come around to listen to it. Crazy shit."

"Edward!" Suzanne scolded. "What is he saying to them?"

The phone rang. It was another neighbor, Caroline Thatcher, the neighborhood's worst gossip and editor of the local community newspaper.

"How'd Buster know the stock market was going to go up 300 points yesterday?" she asked.

"He said *that?*" Suzanne said.

"Yes," Thatcher said.

"And *did* it?"

"Not only that, but the stocks he picked went up exactly as he said they would. Look Suzanne, what's his source?"

"Carrie, don't worry about it. I think he's dreaming it," she said and hung up.

She looked out the kitchen window and saw a delivery truck pull up. It was the local florist delivering arrangements of flowers. Suzanne could see people spreading blankets on their lawn off the side porch. They were pulling up coolers on wheels. They were lighting grills.

She walked out the side porch door.

"Buster, honey, what are these people doing?"

Buster was sitting on the settee, legs still tucked under him. He had a flower chain of jonquils around his neck. Someone had placed elaborate flower arrangements on the porch around the settee. Incense was burning somewhere nearby. One woman Suzanne didn't recognize was sitting at Buster's feet, playing a recorder slowly and quietly.

"They have come unto me," he said and he stretched out his arms above the heads of the growing crowd of neighbors and strangers who looked like they were tailgating in Suzanne's backyard.

"Time," he said to the crowd of people on the lawn, who looked up at Buster intently, "becomes the destroyer. It is a devouring construct of the mercantile death spirit. It is a black shadow that ensnares our souls."

The crowd buzzed excitedly. More and more people were arriving on foot and by car until pretty soon the entire block was gridlocked with traffic. A TV news truck was stuck down at the end of the street and the crew was struggling with their equipment to get up the hill to the house.

Suzanne took out her phone and called Dr. Isherwood. "Yes, we need that appointment we talked about as soon as possible," she told him.

"For the infinite perspective, there is no time." Buster was exhorting the crowd and some people applauded and chanted some strange mantra in unison.

"I'll bring him in tomorrow, then, thank you."

As Suzanne hung up, someone placed a necklace of flowers around *her* neck. People were pushing to get close to Buster.

"I can't see my car," she said to the people crowded around her on the porch. "Can anyone see my car?"

Since Buster wasn't getting much sleep, Suzanne decided to drive him. The psychiatrist was old enough to be Buster's mother and had a terrific head cold the day they went to see her.

Brenda Rose Gustafson sat in a big leather chair and plucked tissues from a box front of her. After Suzanne told Dr. Gustafson about the voices and Buster's strange pronouncements, she tried to get Buster to talk about when the voices first started.

Buster didn't answer. He sat cross-legged on Gustafson's sofa and peered out the window.

Suzanne waited a moment then answered for him. "He said he had a dream about a rooster running around in the front yard," she said. "He stands on the porch trying to get the rooster to come into the house. But it just keeps running in circles in the front yard."

"A running rooster." Dr. Gustafson made some notes.

"You should know," Suzanne said, "that we once had some of those little chicks that you get from the green grocer at Easter time, you know, for the kids. They dye them green and purple, like Easter eggs…"

"Green and purple chicks," Dr. Gustafson said, writing.

"Well, they don't *stay* chicks, of course," Suzanne said. "They turn into, well, they turn into chickens and—a rooster. We had one of them when the twins were little. That may be what Buster was thinking of."

Buster sat in the chair, silent, staring out the window.

Dr. Gustafson looked up over her red nose and her glasses. "And the chick that became a rooster…did it run around in the yard?"

Suzanne smiled. "No, it, um. It got out of the pen through a gap in the fencing Buster had been meaning to fix. It went out into the road and was run over by the Good Humor truck. Mallory and Edward were devastated. Buster blamed himself for a long time, but I told him it wasn't his fault."

"Buster, do you know if the rooster in your dreams was the one that got hit by the truck?" Gustafson said.

Buster sat, his hands folded in front of him.

"Would you like to talk about why you wanted the rooster to come into the house?"

Suzanne shrugged and smiled weakly.

"All right then," Dr. Gustafson said. "But before we finish today, let me ask you: Is there anything you want to say about the voices?"

Buster sat still, only breathing.

Suzanne's eyes were wet. "I just want my husband back. *Somehow.*"

Gustafson closed her notebook, capped her pen. She took Suzanne's hand in a motherly way and smiled. "Try to get some sleep, both of you."

A couple weeks later, when Suzanne went to pick Buster up at the end of his final session, she had a book under her arm.

"What're you reading?" Dr. Gustafson asked.

"Flannery O'Connor," Suzanne said, shrugging and smiling weakly. "Look, there isn't any more science on this. We're at the edge. I've been going through Huxley, Chesterton, T. S. Eliot, some C. S. Lewis. Cock-eyed, religious stuff."

"Any insights?" Dr. Gustafson asked.

"Just a little empathy."

"Sometimes all it takes is time." Gustafson said. "He's making progress. We're talking a lot about his childhood. Did you know he wanted to be a TV announcer when he was a kid?"

Suzanne watched Buster slowly putting on his coat.

She hiked the book and her purse up in her arms, crossing them on her chest. "Sometimes I think our heads, I think his head, gets too full of—crap. Maybe he just needed to let go for a while. Before all this started, we were planning—maybe we should get away together—just us. Hard to have bad thoughts with your feet stuck in the sand, you know? Still, I keep thinking all he has to do is open the door—and let the rooster in! But I know how silly I'm sounding…"

"Not silly at all. Imagination can be a pretty powerful medicine," Gustafson said. "And he *is* getting better, Suzanne. You'll see."

One afternoon just as the weather was starting to turn chilly, the yard had filled with people, like always. A TV helicopter hovered overhead, waiting for Buster to address the multitude.

Suzanne was in the kitchen, watching, making a pot of herbal tea.

Buster, cross-legged on the settee on the side porch, seemed somehow sad and anxious. Some in the crowd, sensing something different this time, began to keen a low, wordless dirge. Soon it spread throughout the crowd and when it reached a crescendo, Buster raised his hands over them, and they fell silent.

He swallowed and began. "A fire in the night means you must hang your clothes with the hooks of the hangers facing inward," he said.

"No!" some in the crowd yelled.

"The fire's flames will be confounded by the *yin*," Buster told them.

The crowd started to become unsettled. People were starting to scream at Buster.

"No! No! You said it was the *yang*! The *yang*!" People were on their feet, shaking their fists at Buster.

"You said to face the hangers outward! You said the thief must struggle with the *yang*!" a young man yelled. He stood, hopped aboard his bicycle, and headed off.

Buster continued. "If you face the hooks in, there will be no struggle with the *yin* to get the clothing out in the fire."

"Hypocrite!" someone yelled at him.

Someone threw a piece of fruit rind, hitting Buster in the shoulder, leaving a stain on his shirt.

Buster rubbed his temples and squinted. "Phooey on the chop suey."

There was a momentary silence, then a loud moan of confusion and disbelief from the crowd.

"'Calgon, take me away,'" Buster said, holding out his hands to them.

Suzanne came to the kitchen window, listening. She started shaking her head and laughing.

"No, no, no! It's the opposite of what you promised!" others yelled.

The young girl who sat at his feet with the recorder stood up and snapped the instrument in two, throwing the pieces in Buster's lap.

"'Pepsi Cola, hits the spot.'" Buster said, tears rolling down his face. "'Twelve full ounces, that's a lot.'"

Suzanne came out onto the side porch with Buster's favorite sweater. She took the necklace of flowers from around his neck and threw it off the porch.

"Fake!" someone yelled.

She put the sweater around his shoulders.

People were folding their blankets and putting out their incense. Cars were pulling away from the driveway and backing down the street. One car revved its engine and spun its wheels, kicking gravel up against the back wall of the garage.

"Be careful pulling out," Buster said.

The TV helicopter hovered for a moment longer to get a final close-up, then peeled off, heading north to check on rush hour traffic along the Jones Falls Expressway.

Tidings

Gus couldn't believe the guy had hit him so hard.

The cheekbone just under his left eye had turned into a hard knob and had just started to smart. It would really hurt later on, but for now he was glad it was cold enough out to keep the swelling down.

Nothing was open on Christmas morning, of course, and it wasn't light out yet. So Gus continued up St. Paul Street looking as if he had an important destination, were on some important mission. He passed the soup kitchen where already a line had formed, lanky gray figures who shuffled and spat, muttering and shivering. Who needed to look tough when the mercury was making trouble?

He'd learned that when he was in the Army in Alaska. That and a lot of Shakespeare and Tennyson. When you're frozen in time on an Army base for two years with nothing but a pool table and a USO library, you learn at least two kinds of English real well.

Gus had learned one of them well enough to pass off fake credentials at a local community college and land a job teaching undergraduate literature courses when he got back. Until they found out.

When Molly got pregnant with Claire, they got married at the courthouse and he took a job on the line at the toothbrush factory in Hampden. They rented a two-bedroom apartment and Molly cut hair at Tanya's while her mother tended to Claire. They were almost making it when Gus started hitting the bars again. That fall, she kicked him out. By Thanksgiving she was seeing a new boyfriend. He held out hope they get back together, until he heard the boyfriend had moved in with her. Then he got served the papers.

A big dump truck rolled by slowly and a burly man in a baseball hat called out to him. It was a guy named Gilbert Gus had befriended in a Fells Point bar who drove for the city department of transit and traffic. Gus had beaten Gilbert at pool every time they played, caging rounds of beer and bourbon until they'd throw him out.

"Hey Gus, gonna need a shotgun man tonight," Gilbert said. "They're calling for six inches and we got that whole stretch of Charles Street to do by tomorrow first light. Easy money, hombre."

Gus didn't look up. He shook his head quickly and ducked down an alley until Gilbert and the salt truck had passed. Shotgun on the nightshift paid fifty bucks. If he didn't drink it up, that'd give him enough to get a hot shower and a shave somewhere. But he didn't feel like talking and he knew an overnight shift with Gilbert in the salt truck would mean having to hold up his end of a conversation he didn't feel like having. All he wanted was ten minutes with Claire and two with Molly to tell her—what? That he was sorry for all the broken promises?

He passed the hooded men in the soup line at St. Elizabeth's, keeping his head turned to the street, hiding his shiner. A crazy glowing plastic Santa up the street screeched out carols, like a Day-Glo siren. Gus made that his destination for the moment. In the twilit morning, it looked like a warm, life-giving thing.

Molly's boyfriend had really socked him. It wasn't like he had asked for money or a bed or anything. But he had wanted to see Claire on Christmas Eve. Custody agreements or no.

"I'll give her the present and I'll go, Moll. I'll give her. Then you give her the package and I'll go. I'm not. Get your hands off me. Drunk. I just want to..."

He fell into a silence so deep, he took it for death.

Then came angels' voices, caroling. They got him up off the steps and steadied him. College kids from the art institute.

"I'm all right. Just a little bump. Thanks. Just a little too much Christmas cheer at the office. My wife'll kill me for tearing that knee out. Yeh, yeh, my package. Thanks. Right. Let heaven and nature."

When he got to the porch with the crazy Santa, he stopped and basked a little in its light. Above the shrill music he heard a startling, familiar sound.

A baby was crying. From the alley off 31st Street, the crying was coming from inside a rusty Dumpster. It's really too cold out for such a thing, he thought. He reached in the open side of the bin and pulled a sheet of newspaper aside. He saw a moving athletic bag. He had to put his palm along a bulge and feel it squirm to satisfy his disbelief.

Sure, he had heard of this. But on Christmas!

He looked up and down the alley. No one shouted. He heard no one running toward him. He put his fingers through the loops of the bag and gingerly lifted it from a cradle of debris, surprised that it weighed about as much as a sack of sugar. There was no sound from the bag except the gentle song of the nylon, as if a tiny set of fingers lightly brushed against it.

He took it to a bench along Guilford Avenue and, just after a bus lumbered by, unzipped the bag. A tiny moon face, appeared, pale blue, yawning. The color shocked him, filling him suddenly with purpose. The squinting liquid eyes searched him. He took off his scarf and tucked it into the bag around the infant. He gently zipped the bag up again, leaving a small opening.

"You're about as blue as I am," Gus told the baby, looking up and down the street for a pay phone.

Mrs. Morowitz had a mustache.

Her heart, however, was a chapter from the Song of Solomon. She had already worked the day shift as head triage nurse in the ER. Then she caught wind of the little shiksa in ER admitting whose mother had just come home for the holiday after a post-menopausal d&c. So she took the night shift, too.

What, they wouldn't do it for you? You know all about d&c firsthand. Besides, you could use the money. Who couldn't? The worst thing—machine coffee. So, you have a slow night...

She was surprised when the phone rang.

"Union Memorial Emergency Admitting. Mrs. Morowitz speaking."

"We want to talk to a doctor."

"Who's we? You playing with the symphony, pal?"

"He's very cold. He's—well—he's blue."

Mrs. Morowitz took the glasses that dangled on a silver chain over her bosom and placed them on the tip of her nose.

"Let me guess. He was right under the tree—next to the tequila?"

"No, it's nothing like that. It's a baby. Listen, is there a doctor?"

"Of course, there are doctors. You have reached a hospital." Mrs. Morowitz decided this was not just another drunken Christmas Eve reveler.

"What I need to know is, can you help me? I mean, I don't want any trouble."

"Helping you is no trouble, sir. Did you say the baby is blue? Where are you?"

"I'm standing outside, next to the taxi stand."

"Then I would suggest that by all means you come inside, young man."

Gus hung up and walked through a big set of automatic doors. He was bathed in warm white light. It smelled like the Christmases of his childhood, like pine trees and tangerines.

He was met by a fat little gray-haired woman with a clipboard and glasses on the end of her nose. Gus unzipped the athletic bag, held out the handles and said, "Can you do anything?"

"Follow me," Mrs. Morowitz said. She grabbed a phone and yelled something. They took the bag and shoved him along a corridor off the emergency waiting room. A soft bonging started in the hallway that reminded Gus of a doorbell. Several people in scrubs appeared and just as quickly disappeared. Everything was a whirl for a long time.

The next thing he knew he was sitting opposite Mrs. Morowitz. It was quiet again, and he had his hands wrapped around a cup of coffee. She was working antiseptic into the wound under his eye.

"It's a good one. Pretty close to being open. So you, what did she do first, the crying or the hitting?"

"It wasn't like that. It was her boyfriend. I wanted to see my little girl. That package was for her."

"Quite a homecoming. Been away long?"

"A year without talking. Then a year with lots of shouting."

"Look, it's never black and white, but can you blame her? You *did* run out, didn't you? Hold still."

He was sorry he had told her so much. "I was self-medicating," Gus said softly.

She continued to dress the contusion. "A man once said every happy family is happy the same. Every unhappy family is unhappy different."

"Sounds like—Tolstoy." he said.

"It is. But a rabbi I know thinks he thought it up."

"He's the smartest rabbi I ever heard of."

"Point is, you got tied up with two unhappy families this morning. Yours," she said, finishing the bandage and nodding towards the nursery. "And his. You tell me."

"He's got about as much of a chance as I do—"

"Sarah."

"Gus," he said, shaking her hand.

"I don't believe you, Gus," she said, handing him a clipboard to sign. She looked at it as he got up. "Hey, there's no last name here, Gus."

He swallowed hard, suddenly afraid. "I don't want any trouble. I haven't worked in four months. Haven't talked to my little girl in-—"

He put his hand over his eyes. The next thing, she was slowly hugging him, his face nearly buried in her grey hair.

"Listen. You're a smart guy! You did a big thing last night. You went home. And you did another one this morning. You saved his life, for crying out loud! What—they have to pin a medal on you for you to see it? He's gonna' make it. But you? Come here."

She led him to the nursery. They picked out the bassinet with the foundling under a heat lamp. He was pink and crying, thrashing his legs in the air.

"Got lungs like my son, the sportscaster," Mrs. Morowitz said.

Gus pulled the package from his big coat pocket and handed it to her.

"Can you see he gets it? It's a dog—or a bear, I don't know. I stole it." He shrugged a laugh and shook his head. "Merry Christmas," he said and started to walk away.

"Not so fast, mister. We have a tradition around here." Gus turned, searching her eyes. She stared at him over those glasses on her nose. "You bring in a foundling, you help take care of him," she said, pen poised above the clipboard.

Gus looked at the infant.

"Well, you at least have a name for him, don't you?"

"If his trip is going to be anything like mine—better call him 'Ulysses'."

"You sure? These things stick, you know."

Gus studied the tiny pink face again and half smiled at the little woolen Santa's cap they had put on him.

"No. Call him Nick," Gus said, taking a step forward and pointing through the glass at the baby. "Merry Christmas, Nick."

"'Nick' it is. I'll tell Social Services to make sure they write this one down," Mrs. Morowitz said. "And don't mistake my meaning, but I don't ever want to see either of you anywhere near this place again. Get it?"

Gus looked up and saw the snow falling outside the big glass ER doors. It was starting to stick on 33rd Street and all up and down Charles Street. He heard a big diesel rumble and clatter by, its chains beating out industrial strength "Jingle Bells" on the pavement.

"Got it," Gus said, smiling for the second time on Christmas, wondering if Gilbert would stop for his ten o'clock coffee at the Sip & Bite, like always. He just had to tell somebody the good news.

There Angels Dance

The postulant got out of bed in the dark and shivered as he pulled a knit cap over his close-cropped hair. He tucked his scapular into his t-shirt and put on a pair of running shorts and a hoodie with the seminary's logo across the front. Then he paused, removed the scapular, folded it carefully, and placed it under the lamp on the bureau in their room. *Our dog tags*, Scanlan had joked at their first meeting as roommates. He skipped socks and tied on his running shoes.

Scanlan was snoring softly as he pulled closed the door of their suite. He walked out of the dormitory into the darkness across the lawn and down the long brick sidewalk toward the iron gates. While the morning air was cool and the first frost had not yet come, he watched his breath come out in big clouds. The air was crisp and dry, smelled of spice from the leaves on the lawn. Turning right out of the seminary drive and stretching briefly, he started jogging down Roland Avenue toward the city.

Small and powerfully built, dark-haired and olive-skinned, he had blushed when the others nicknamed him "Romeo." He said nothing in protest, so they kept it up. They'd also had passed around a rusty-stapled carbon copy of sections of Kramer's translation of the Gilgamesh saga, the parts that spoke of Lilith, demon-woman, bird spirit, corrupter, seducer, and later first wife and tempter of Adam, before Eve. Essential reading for a priest-to-be, Scanlan assured him when he smuggled it into their room in a dog-eared folder the day before the literature test on Macbeth. Tall, redheaded, and full of mischief, Scanlan constantly needled his little roommate about his overly studious nature. Was Scalan intending academic sabotage? He couldn't help poring over the Kramer text all that night.

The charge of nerdiness was true. Saturday evenings, when they'd all pile in the van and go drinking in Charles Village, he'd stay behind to struggle with geometry–Euclid and parallel lines, Lobachevsky and the horosphere, Hjelmslev transformations. But lately, he'd been finding it more and more difficult to keep his mind on it—the work, the books, on prayer. *Lord, I am not worthy. Say but the word…*

Running at dawn, he found, had been the best tonic for his spirit. As he ran this morning, the sun was just coming up along the Jones Falls Valley, turning the hillsides of already butternut leaves into swathes of bright gold. He continued to run, turning right and heading along 41st Street, watching his shadow slowly elongate, then as he passed under each streetlight, quickly snap back into his feet. He could feel the tension and resistance of the first steps, the first mile, and then the warm suffusion through his lungs and muscles as he found the pace, his breathing regular and slow, his stride growing rhythmic.

As he passed a group of high school runners—Gilman boys by their shirts, stoic in their own morning workout— memories from high school flooded his mind.

When she entered his mind each day, Gwen's freckles were what he always remembered most. How her face and arms and back were covered in a field of peach speckles. And where the freckles weren't, she had smooth, cream-colored skin he couldn't get out of his mind now. She had laughed when he told her he was starting the process that might lead to his entering the priesthood. It's like getting married, he told her. They had exchanged rings in high school, full well knowing that college would be the end. He had given Gwen her ring back that night. He wanted her to keep his, even though she knew his heart had changed, and that he could give her nothing else that would last besides the ring and his promise of fidelity. They watched a great blue heron patiently fishing in the cold stream below Lake Roland. He took her hand. I want you to see other people, he told her. And then she cried because she knew there would be lots of other people in her life at college in New York. They both knew that was true.

I love you, Tim.

I love *you*, Gwen.

Suddenly she flung her ring into the Jones Falls, below the dam.

There now, she said crying, her eyes like wet emeralds, I'm married to you and to the Jones Falls.

It sent a shiver through him and he pondered the imponderable: Would they know each other—love each other–in heaven? Would they be allowed a great celestial do-over? What did Augustine say about heaven?

It was as if a colossal starting gun had been fired on graduation day, and they all took off in a zigzagging Easter egg hunt in every direction toward their futures–law, medical school, banking, architecture, the military, chemical engineering, marriage, parenthood—and what about a vocation in the church? Fr. Miller had described it to him as getting married—was it really all that different? Forswear all others. But not yet, not yet. His novitiate was still a full year ahead.

Mr. Hall, his high school track coach, had subtly mocked his decision. There's no Vatican Olympic Team, he said. You placed in the states. You could go all the way. *All the way*—where? he thought.

Fr. Miller, his Confessor, had gently reminded him of Augustine's claim that he would choose to become a "vessel of wrath or a vessel of mercy." Poverty, obedience, chastity.

"You are merely trying to discern your vocation," Fr. Miller had told him. "It's too early; we don't want you yet. If you said yes tomorrow, you could not take vows. Doubts are natural. Live your life. Get out in the world. Read the literature, the scripture. And pray—if you like. Watch for signs— and they're easy to spot. See what strikes you and reflect on why."

But the flesh is not weak; the flesh is strong, the old priest had said. Your soul is a fortress. The Adversary will find and attack the weakest gate into the citadel. Consider that martyrs and saints are not those who are super-human, not god-like. Saints are those with the strength to be human for just one moment longer than everyone else.

The first thing that had stuck with him about life in the seminary had been ridiculously mundane: the stiffness of the clean white sheets with that vaguely burned smell from the big institutional dryers downstairs. And the heaviness of the coffee at breakfast as if the urn had been left on all night.

He had written—thanks to roommate Scalan and the Kramer text—an exegesis for his first term literature class on Keats's "La Belle Dame Sans Merci." The femme fatale was ubiquitous in art, he argued, citing Lady Macbeth, Goethe's *Faust's* Helen, and Mae West. She lacks pity because she lacks all semblance of humanity. The eternal feminine—while indeed "drawing us on"—was at best disinterested, he concluded and not convincingly. He received a grade of C- and a chiding note from the professor to try to be more original next time.

At St. Mary's he had been quickly immersed, swimming around what he did not understand. After philosophy class his head always felt like box full of coat hangers. He told Fr. Miller, who said he needed to sort out the difficulties, one by one. Discriminate. Discern. Decide. Aristotle was knotty. Plato opaque. Descartes contradictory. Only Pascal intrigued him with the Wager: whether there's a God or not, believing stacks the odds in your favor. In ethics class, they asked them to write down on a piece of paper five things in answer to the question: "What would you die for?" His list read: "self, family, country, beliefs, home." A Roman collar? His faith? Could he die for his faith?

He ran onto the 41st Street Bridge where it spanned the gulf of air over the Jones Falls Expressway, an eight-lane main artery divided by a Jersey wall. Traffic at this time of day was already steady, building toward rush hour. The bridge had long been decommissioned by the city when it re-mapped Druid Hill Park and it was now a wide foot and bike path with high chain link fences on either side that kept people from tossing things down onto the expressway traffic.

Every morning that fall when he had come this way, he passed the place on the safety fence facing the southbound lanes where someone had come along and laboriously cut a swath through the fencing to about three feet high, creating an opening wide enough to squeeze through a small body. Two strong people must have held the third person who had leaned out over the traffic to scrawl with a can of red spray paint in three-foot-high letter-ing on the bridge the misspelled message for thousands of daily southbound commuters: "Suppot Our Troop." He had seen the message a dozen times from the shuttle they took from the seminary down to the soup kitchen at the Franciscan Center, and on the days they went to the city jail to tutor the inmates or help their families with their tax forms or leases. The message was scrawled in a flat space just above a lighted, LED sign that exhorted motor-ists to "report any suspicious activity to the Department of Transit and Traf-fic" by calling the 1-800 number.

He trotted up the slight incline that gave onto the bridge and was startled to see the woman first, standing, facing the southbound traffic, one hand casually cradling her big black handbag, the other at her side. Then he saw the boy standing in front of her. They were standing at the split in the safety fence. The little boy was nosing what looked like a rock or a piece of concrete about the size of softball out through the split, onto the bridge truss. The woman was looking down at him and—he couldn't believe it—*smiling.* Was she his mother? Sister? Nanny? Some crazy aunt?

She was slender, beautiful, with short dark hair. She was wearing a short dark skirt, a black leather jacket with fringe, and hoop earrings. There was something strangely familiar about her. Hadn't he seen her a dozen—a hundred—times in the bars in Fells Point and Charles Village and Canton? And yet he had never known her. He felt that something about her entered him, like the feeling of catching a cold—and knowing it was there, like she was some viral, reaching presence.

She was speaking to the little boy softly. She didn't look up as he approached them. The boy was about six or seven, bundled up in a thick quilted coat with a scarf and an earmuff hat and gloves. He continued to push the rough sphere of rock toward the edge of the bridge truss with his foot.

She continued to talk to him softly.

He had almost reached where they stood, almost cried out Hey! as the tip of the boy's foot finally, timidly, nudged the piece of stone off the truss down onto the morning commuter traffic on the expressway.

He felt himself instinctively lunge for the safety fence, as if grabbing the links with both fists could pull back the plummeting rock.

He pulled himself up and looked down at the rock, as it appeared to drop in slow motion. A silver Lexus and the rock came together in almost what seemed to him then like an animated ballet. According to Lobachevsky, two parallel lines could converge on the surface of the horosphere, a sphere with its center at infinity.

He never saw the driver's face. On the car's windshield appeared a large, white, crystalline splash, blossoming slowly from where he stood like a handful of paint or a giant bird shit. He turned and strode across the bridge to see the car coming out from under on the other side, weaving lazily at first, then more crazily, until it spun completely around and—in a terrific explosion of metal and glass—was struck head on by a large pickup truck full of Latino men. The men were screaming and flying in slow motion and several disappeared into the crush of traffic, appearing to be gobbled up by on-rushing cars and trucks.

He heard a banshee-wail of brakes below.

His heart raced and, panting, he looked at the boy and woman. He could not force himself to speak to them. The boy stood motionless, looking down, his hands splayed out to his sides like a high diver's ready stance. The woman looked at the chaos unfolding below them for a moment and then looked up directly at him. *She was smiling*! When her eyes locked with his, she grinned. Her teeth were perfect. He felt hot in her gaze. Thoughts like hailstones beat in his head, alarming, final. He could help them—or find them help at the Franciscan Center or at the House of Ruth. He would ask the Provincial to lend her rent or mortgage—whatever they needed.

Already the emergency vehicles' sirens wailed and they were stacking up on the highway shoulders under the footbridge for a quarter mile on each side, medics tending to the victims of the crashes, firemen spraying foam on the wrecks, police closing the interstate down on both north- and southbound lanes. He could hear the far away beating of helicopter blades, rapidly coming closer.

He instantly became aware that the boy was almost through the separation in the safety fence, that another step and he would fall the fifty feet to the roadway, where the traffic wreckage lay snarled. Police sirens whooped and oscillated until they harmonized into a thumping mass of red and blue air beneath them.

She stared and him, smiling with the perfect white teeth, the red lips, the laughing eyes, the beautiful blush of her cheeks. He knew her and had never met her.

In his peripheral vision, the dark silhouettes of the SWAT team sharpshooters darted into view at each end of the footbridge, ducking and weaving, trying to see the three people on the bridge and their relative positions: the little boy, the stylishly dressed, grimacing woman behind him, the small, dark-skinned man standing near them. Did he have a weapon? Was the woman hysterical—it was difficult for them to tell.

He could hear the sizzle of their radios–their mutterings. He was sure he had been sighted by several high-powered rifles by now and thought he saw a busy swarm of three or four tiny red dots from their laser sights dancing across his chest exactly where his heart was beating. He held his hands out from his sides, his palms flat and facing the ground, like the boy's, in the diver's ready stance. He stood perfectly still, facing the woman.

"Freeze! Don't you move a muscle!" a man screamed from the end of the footbridge. "Both ends are blocked! Lie down on the ground—do it NOW!"

He and the boy looked at her. She smiled the smile again, that smile.

"Jump," she said to the two of them. It seemed somehow insanely logical.

"I'll go," the boy said softly without looking up.

"No!" he screamed at them and moved toward the jagged cut opening in the safety fence.

Then the sharpshooters took him.

As Scanlan and the others came down at seven thirty, they could hear the phone ringing in the Rector's office off the wide marble foyer.

Scanlan paused, looking back up the huge mahogany staircase before going in to lauds and breakfast.

Enough witnesses down on the highway surface looking up at the bridge swore they saw the man with the woman and the child hold out his arms as if somehow shielding them from the dark-armored police that the story began to circulate as rumor, then as gossip, then as urban legend. For a time, no one knew quite what had happened for sure.

But media reports said the witnesses were too far away, at the wrong angle, and had had it all wrong. It had all been just a confluence of accidents. Still, as the story was retold, some people said that, in saving the woman and the child, he must have been a hero or a saint or something else—remembered, as in a dream, from their childhoods.

"And Little Lambs Eat Ivy"

During the first week of her first term teaching kindergarten at Elmwood Elementary School, her principal congratulated Miss Pembroke on her joining the faculty.

"We're so delighted to have you," Mrs. Echodale told her. "You are our very first Wiccan faculty member. As you know, we're very committed to incorporating diverse cultures into our community here at Elmwood. Your being among us does *so* much for our diversity ratios."

Miss Pembroke smiled demurely.

"Honestly, we can't *wait* for Halloween," Mrs. Echodale said, clasping her hands in front of her face. "Did anyone ever tell you—oh they *must* have—that you look the absolute image of Gwyneth Paltrow?"

Miss Pembroke blushed and nodded slightly. "I get that a lot," she said.

At Halloween, Miss Pembroke, against the advice of her coven mother, dressed as Snow White and carried a basket of apples throughout the day. She told Mrs. Echodale, who was mildly confused, that white witches didn't dress in black and ride broomsticks. The older woman shrugged and asked the younger if an evergreen tree in the kindergarten for the holidays would meet with her approval.

"Oh, yes, a tree at the holidays is perfectly Druidic. We adore them," Miss Pembroke said.

And so Thanksgiving and Christmas came and went—much to the relief of her students' parents— with Pilgrim pageants and snowmen and caroling around the piano.

By late January, Miss Pembroke felt as if she held them in thrall and began to think that teaching might not be such a bad career choice for her after all. She felt accepted by the students, parents, and faculty alike, and was glad the inclusive atmosphere at Elmwood tolerated her occasional absences for Wiccan feast days.

Soon it would be spring and soon she'd be getting married. Her initial trepidation at marrying not only outside the coven, but outside Wicca had subsided. Todd was like a big goofy Teddy bear when they talked honeymoon and buying their first condo. He was never more smitten and she was never more in love. She loved him even more because he was so accepting of her different ways.

"It's today–today!" the children whispered and giggled to each other as they hung up their coats and mittens in the cloak room in back of Miss Pembroke's kindergarten. By the time the little hand on the big wooden clock had reached ten, the sunny warren of the schoolroom was near brimming over with anticipation. The weak February sun slanted through the windows and threw fuzzy shadows along the brightly decorated bulletin boards.

"It's today!" their tiny eyes said to one another across the polished floor filled with mats at naptime.

Miss Pembroke softly clapped her hands. "Story time!"

They quickly folded their mats and everyone scurried for a good seat near the piano bench. One little girl stood near the art supply shelves and began to cry.

"Miss Pembroke! Robert Groughman keeps putting gum in my hair!" Miss Pembroke smiled and walked through the throng of anxious faces to the little girl, who pointed dourly at Robert. He stood, back to her, looking out the long row of windows.

Now, she thought, it was time again for a lesson on The Golden Rule. Halfway through her first year with the kindergarten she still marveled at how adaptable, how malleable they were!

Don't smile until Christmas, Mrs. Echodale had warned her. *Firmness with kindness is the rule of the day*, the older woman had said. Miss Pembroke just nodded and smiled. How difficult could dealing with five and six year-olds be?

She approached Robert Groughman, next to where the pea plant garden was struggling.

"Robert, would you like it if someone stuck something on you?"

The boy shook his head and pushed out his lower lip, histrionically. He sulked disingenuously for a moment, then veered past her towards the building blocks, yodeling.

"Miss Pembroke!" Several girls chased after her, pulling her arms, her dress.

The class gathered in a semicircle around her. She sat on a low stool and read from a big cardboard storybook about a turtle party in Turnip Village.

One small boy up front sat low and directly in front of Miss Pembroke, and accidentally saw the twenty-four-year-old's bikini underwear. He was speechless.

When the turtle party was over, Miss Pembroke read a story about a robot with wheels for feet. The robot couldn't play like other children. The robot exhibited anti-social behavior until he met a friendly tinsmith. The tinsmith was the hero of the story and the children clapped when he gave the robot metal feet.

By the end of the second story, the play clock was about to announce the hour again. They could subdue their excitement no longer.

One tiny girl, standing on the foredeck of the play tugboat, let out a shriek. Everyone started squealing at once.

"Is he here yet? Miss Pembroke, can we see him now?"

The young woman smiled as the mob of children pressed around her. Some of them milled about aimlessly.

"Yes, yes, he'll be here soon. And we all know what he does. He looks for his–"

"Shadow!" They all cried in unison.

"And if he sees it, he goes back underground for six more weeks of–"

"Winter! Winter!" they chanted.

"Very good!" She laughed at their squeaks and fitful dancing.

One boy ran to the xylophone and began banging out a cacophonous overture. Miss Pembroke led a group of the children to the incubator full of small hens' eggs. She hoped to distract them, or channel their nervousness into a lesson.

"See how warm and cozy they are? What will happen in a little while?"

"Hatch! Hatch! They'll hatch, Miss Pembroke!" they intoned.

One boy peered into the incubator window and rocked the box. "Hatch! Hatch!" he muttered like an incantation.

"Now John, don't wake up the baby chicks before they're finished sleeping!"

At fifteen after three, there was a knock at the door. Everyone froze. All eyes turned to the young woman.

"Bobby, will you see who that is, please?"

The boy labored to open the big door and a tall young man stepped into the room.

"Children, I promised you that since today is Groundhog Day, we would be visited by a groundhog. And here he is." She smiled and the man smiled. There was a collective gasp of small breaths.

"He's not a groundhog, Miss Pembroke, he's a *person*!"

"Groundhogs are furry, Miss Pembroke!"

"You said we would see a groundhog!"

She laughed and took the man by the hand.

"This is *my* groundhog, and his name is Todd Burton."

One of the twins started bawling inconsolably. The boy at the xylophone took up his playing again, this time in an anguished dirge.

"Awwww, Miss Pembroke," said one girl with a head full of blonde curls, "You said a *real, live* groundhog!"

It was true, she realized; she had pulled a mean trick. She would make it up to them after the spring vacation with a field trip to the zoo, she thought.

But the day ended with their displeasure hanging in the air, like chalk dust.

"Now, let's get our hats and coats and mittens and lunch pails. Let's see who can be the quietest in lining up!"

When the troop had disappeared into the cloakroom, Todd gave Miss Pembroke a kiss.

"He *kissed* her!" one of them whispered from the crack in the cloakroom door.

And they never trusted her again.

Miss Pembroke married in the spring, and one morning, she sat in bed, with the bright May sun streaming through the curtains. Todd was completely buried beneath a big comforter.

The phone rang. It was her coven mother.

"Is everything all right?" the coven elder asked.

"Yes, things are just so—well, as you can imagine—different now."

"We were worried about you," the coven mother said.

"I'm *fine*," Mrs. Burton-née-Pembroke said.

"You should know that the condo association board passed a motion last night stipulating that non-Wiccans won't be allowed to buy in. They're even checking coven pedigrees. Can you believe it? You and Todd didn't sign a contract yet, did you? You might want to reconsider going through all that."

"Todd isn't a non-Wiccan…he's just a, he's just a…" She looked at the big form under the blankets. "He's a big *schnoopie*. He's *my* big schnoopie!" she said, laughing. "We'll be *fine*."

"Listen, sweetie, stay in touch, OK?" The older witch said good-bye and hung up.

She sipped her mug of tea.

"Todd?" The quilt did not move.

"Dear, how do you think I should break it to them. About my name being different now?"

He stirred under the covers and made an inarticulate sound.

"Honey?"

From the corner of her eye, she saw his head emerge from beneath the quilt, and for an instant, mistook it.

Grizzled, squinting in the light, he had been transformed. She shivered violently and the illusion vanished. But in her distraction that morning she burned the eggs and would not come out of the kitchen until she was sure he was safely enclosed in the shower.

The Perfect Pancake

The sun and its flaky crust of clouds on the evening horizon reminded her so much of peach cobbler that she was sure now there would be one on the table Thanksgiving Day, right alongside the pumpkin pie. She'd have whortleberry turnovers for dessert, too, if she could get them in season. She owed Clarissa that much.

Meanwhile, he was forward in the sails, fooling with the jib halyard, and kept shouting back through the flailing nylon things like, "Ready about! Let go the sheets! Steady, steady!" Her attention snapped back to the tiller in her hands and the fact that, to make way in light air sometimes you have to deliberately knock down your sails to catch a different course.

Buster, the captain and her husband (always in that order on their boat), unjammed the problem in the rigging and turned to her with his face drawn in anger. She wondered, as she always had, why men seemed to hate the things they loved to do, and why, for example, golf clubs got bent.

"Hard a'lee. Bring her about!"

Suzanne pulled the tiller hard up and towards her breast. She felt the mysterious weight of the iron keel swing and pull with the same momentum and concussion as a pain of labor.

"Trim the sheet!" He leapt along the rigging towards the helm while she grabbed at the slack rope. Why they called the ropes and lines on a boat sheets, she didn't know. It seemed sensible to her that the sails ought to be called sheets and that they had it backwards, but that was another characteristic of the way men did things.

He jumped into the cockpit beside her and in a moment had everything shipshape. They were running true and fast.

Everything had gone perfectly that weekend, if you disregarded the almost studied vexation he showed, the calling of various parts of the boat vile names under his breath, all of which showed anyway what a good time he was having.

They had left Annapolis on Saturday morning at sunrise, just as the stars were beginning to wink off like the running lights of the scattered fleet out on the water. Their course was for St. Michaels, farther south on the Bay, and all that day they had lazily zigged and zagged across the Chesapeake, with Buster periodically going berserk in the rigging. The fact that this trip was in celebration of their twenty-four years married was tacit, a silent congratulation they offered each other. At one point, Buster did admit that he couldn't remember being happier, and this she took as perhaps the only benediction she would hear on the whole trip.

She was sorry when she had to ruin the mood that afternoon, but she had promised herself she would tell him that weekend, and in handing him a cold beer, she decided to hand him the news with it.

She sat down beside him in the cockpit, and as his arm went around her, she began.

"I wanted to talk to you about that phone call from Clarissa."

"You've mentioned that call three times now and you still haven't told me what she said. Are things all right at school?"

"Everything's fine. What she really called to tell us was that she's coming home for Thanksgiving—" He was looking away, out across the waves. "—With a friend."

"A friend?"

"It's a lover."

"Oh, for God's sake," he said. She shivered and waited for him to continue. "She's only been in school for two months and here she's jumping in the sack with the first Joe College—and he's got three varsity letters, I'll bet. What do they call that—hooking up?"

"I'm not so sure of that, sweetheart."

"Well, let's be frank with her, Suzanne, there'll be none of their doing the laundry while they're under our roof—agreed?" 'Doing the laundry' was the euphemism they used for sex. They had borrowed it from a joke, when she was carrying Edward.

"There's one other thing."

"I can't believe it. Two months and already my daughter is involved with someone. An upperclassman, no doubt."

"Well, no."

"No? Is it worse than that?"

"It's a girl."

She thought that the words had hit him like a squall. He was quiet for a long time. He looked at a channel marker without blinking as they passed it.

"I will talk to Edward and Mallory." His voice sounded piped and funny.

She started to cry and couldn't help it.

He was looking far off in the distance, towards the harbor at St. Michaels.

"Edward," he said again, "we'll have to tell him before they arrive."

She looked astern while their wake was stirring the water into whirlpools. As it grew into evening, she could see the luminescent plankton and noctiluca shimmering as they were drawn into the eddies of the wake and buffeted. Neither of them spoke for a long while.

On the day Clarissa and her friend were to come home, Buster was up early on the roof, thrashing out the inside of the chimney with a chain and letting Edward repeatedly drop a weighted bolt of chicken wire down. He had promised her he'd clean it long before now, and it really didn't matter to her that it hadn't been done; what amazed her was that he picked the dirtiest, most aggravating job around the house on the day their daughter was coming home. She thought that he was up there talking to Edward about Clarissa's coming.

Edward appeared in the kitchen doorway at lunchtime looking like he had been hit and dragged by a leaking oil truck.

As she was putting some sandwiches into a bag, he studied the row of spice jars above the sink.

"Mom, why is Dad afraid I'm going to turn into a little fairy?"

She nearly dropped her fist through the bottom of the bag.

"Did he say that?"

"I was talking about the game this Friday when all of a sudden he said that I'd better not be afraid to walk around in the showers naked or I'd turn into a little fairy."

"Oh," she said, and cupped her hands on his lean face. He was a short boy for his age, but stocky and well-coordinated. She knew that his whole life he had been a modest soul and that the remark had left him baffled.

"What your father is saying, honey, is that he loves you very much and he wants you to grow into a fine strong man like the fine young man you are." Somehow the words tasted like betrayal on her lips, of Clarissa and of herself, and she didn't know why. She gave him the lunch and a thermos of lemonade and sent him off again up the ladders they had set up on the roof of the garage and the gabled roof of the house.

When they came in to clean up for dinner, they were both quiet. Throughout the quick meal, Suzanne and Buster repeated the plans for the evening, all carefully constructed around Clarissa's arrival.

"We will go to the airport and get them," Buster said.

"Mallory's sleeping over at a friend's house. You stay here and hold the fort," she said to Edward.

"Then we'll meet them and bring them back here," Buster said.

"You're sleeping on the basement rollaway, " she interjected. "Clarissa has your room, and her friend will take Clarissa's room."

"Then we come back here and have a pre-Thanksgiving party," Buster said.

"And I don't say a word about 'Rissa's being funny with her friend," Edward blurted.

She gasped lightly. Buster closed his eyes, stood motionless, as if dead.

"And you don't say anything about Clarissa's private affairs," Suzanne told him, putting her hand on the barked roughness of his hand.

She kept running reels of images of the coming three days through her mind, searching for awkward moments, scenarios in which Buster or Edward used his tongue for a shoehorn, but it all seemed surreal and cloudy to her on the way to the airport.

Somehow, as she looked over at Buster, she felt like a celestial body ripping out of its orbit, moving off into a void and dark, or perhaps that this whole thing had polarized their relationship and they were flipping like magnets, away from each other.

When she saw her at the terminal, she felt giddy with the novelty of the whole thing, and pulled free of Buster's arm to hug them both. Aside from being a bit taller and thinner than Clarissa, Anne was her picture in coloring and facial structure. She thought it uncanny and mysterious. But Buster's face was fixed with a nondescript smile.

The three of them talked and cut up all the way back up the Baltimore-Washington Expressway while Buster drove and glared at signs as if he didn't know where he was going.

Without a warning, he came alive and suggested that they go somewhere for a drink before going home.

"We told Edward we'd come right back home, darling."

"That's no problem, since I hold him he could have Lenny and Spud over, and that if we were late he could spend the night at their house."

She felt like she was hearing another language. She said, "That's nice," and then quickly asked Anne if her parents minded her spending Thanksgiving in a strange city.

They had some drinks in town and the girls laughed a lot. Buster finally got them home late. The house was lit up and the TV was still on, but Edward was not up. An annihilated pizza sat on the kitchen table along with many empty soda bottles and a video football game still on the kitchen TV. After checking the basement, Buster came up and announced that all three boys had fallen asleep downstairs with their phones on, apparently trying to wheedle one another into texting girls.

When the house was dark and they had all gone to bed, she began to run the next day's reel through her head. She stopped the motion every time Buster opened his mouth to speak. She carefully edited out his remarks and ran the reel through again.

She was surprised when Buster spoke in the darkness. He had been awake all the time, had probably been making movies all his own.

"I can't help it, Suzanne, but it's such a god-awful kick in the ass. I don't think this is ever going to make sense to Edward."

With that, she pinched him under the covers, hard.

"You stop it now. Stop it."

He shut up and rolled over.

Flickering in his mind, she thought, was the scintillating and impossible vision of his daughter in a snow-white wedding dress with a dark-haired midshipman or an egghead medical student on her arm. For her own peace of mind, she had already edited that scene.

She woke up before he did and lay there listening in the growing daylight. She had to put the turkey in. Someone was stirring downstairs in the kitchen. She could hear bowls and flatware commingling, refrigerator doors sounds, padded and bare feet hitting the tiles. What unearthly mess she would find there later she didn't know, but in her imagination she saw Edward, Lenny, and Spud in full breakfast revelry.

She quickly showered and dressed in jeans and one of Buster's white shirts. She stopped in the hallway and peeked in Edward's room. Clarissa was still sleeping. She peeked in Clarissa's room, was surprised to find the bed empty.

She heard their laughter from the kitchen. She made her way downstairs quietly.

Around the table she saw them, napkins at their necks and milk moustaches painting their upper lips, clanking everything metal against everything made of glass: the three boys, devouring a big, sloppy pancake breakfast.

Anne, standing at the sink, watching them eat and sipping a cup of coffee, seemed embarrassed when Suzanne came into the kitchen.

"Hope I haven't overstepped my welcome," she said.

"H'ray!" said the three boys in unison through mouths full. They meant it as a compliment, that Anne shouldn't feel out of place or embarrassed.

Suzanne started laughing and couldn't stop. She laughed even harder when she found herself half hoping he would slip in the shower and break something.

Whortleberry turnovers, for dessert, she thought. Whortleberry turnovers, for sure.

The Bluebird of Happiness

In twenty years of smoking, Ed Foote had never lit a cigarette on the wrong end. He looked down his nose now, along the paper tube to the scorched filter, hanging there like a bee ready to sting him in the face. A bead of perspiration skied down his nose and jumped onto the cigarette, wetting it through.

Maybe smoking in bed was a bad idea after all, he thought. Besides, she had tossed her matches clear across the room into a plate of half-eaten cheesecake. She rolled over next to him now and put her blond head on his bicep, which was going to fat and covered with gray hair.

"You smell like starch," she told him sleepily before they made love again, before he put his palms on the sides of her pelvis that was so white that he imagined she had just been taken out of the crate, like some sort of Chinese vase.

"Sometimes the shirts–they get that way when you wash them at the Laundromat," he said.

"Do you meet the other women in the Laundromat?" Foote figured she knew there were others because of the things that had collected in a carton under his bathroom sink.

"No, just housewives, usually, nobody special," he said. They were the safest, he thought. "Just housewives who take my quarters and give me nickels and dimes. All of them do it. Even the ones who flirt." He remembered the red-headed wife of the retail executive. He remembered the hot afternoons behind the pool palisade before her kids got home from school. He thought of how he once went to give blood just to get the free test and how those women, desperately, never wanted to know much about him.

"What about me?" She pulled the eiderdown straight across her chest, clamped it tightly under her arms. She was a little chunkier than he liked, but she was perky and athletic. Maybe it was her own feigned modesty that delighted Foote, who at forty-five was still shocked in a happy way that women walked up to him in bars and speculated that he must be a lawyer or something. *Yes, or something, he'd say, I'm a svengali, a defrocked archbishop, a deep-sea diver, and in a few hours you'll be calling me "papa."*

Foote didn't own such things as a lighter or wristwatch, and didn't even carry a cell phone, finding it pleasant instead to rely on others for the amenities of a light or messages or the time of day. It worked in his favor in social situations; whereas men usually thought he was a harmless boob, women thought he was charming. For some magical reason, when they realized he was pretending to be helpless, they were under his power. And he had discovered it worked on younger women best.

"What about me?" she said, insisting.

Her question was the same as all the others'. Foote dabbled in trying to figure out what women really wanted.

But he couldn't be bothered with what women *said* they wanted: flowers at work, trimmed beards and mustaches, fidelity, big shoulders and hands, exotic bath oils, manageable hair, home and hearth, tender embraces over orgasms, orgasms over faking it, soft elbows and knees, little notes and brandy, dignity in the marketplace, anything made of Moroccan leather, children with monosyllabic Anglo-Saxon names, lovers with names full of long vowels, deep tans, a trustworthy mechanic, eye contact, slender waists and buttocks on men, diamond pendants, someone to listen, thick steamy novels for the beach, secret meeting places if married, lurid scenes in public if not, candy and flowers, flowers and champagne, floral print sundresses, light, space, ferns, intelligence in men, humor in men, artistic fingers, rainy day shopping trips, no-worry birth control, equal pay for equal work, waterproof eye make-up that is, wrap-around skirts that do, halters that don't, someone who can fix things, autonomy, stuffed animals, original poems with their names in them, no-stick cooking surfaces, candle-lit Greek cuisine, shoes that stay in style and don't hurt, an extra hour of sleep, compliments from other women, salad lunches, bobbins, bangles, babies, black lace, and business suits.

It all came in one simultaneous deluge that threatened to wash out the bridge to What Women Really Wanted.

"Well, of course, you're different," he said, lying again.

"How different?"

And that was another thing: explanations. *Good Lord–maybe that was it!* Everything explained in completely objective terms. Maybe women wanted– more than sentimentality–A World in Which Things Could Be Made to Make Sense.

The sheer furious novelty of it excited him.

"You might think about it in terms of a soap opera," Foote said. "You know the kind. They are full of good people and bad people."

"And how they're always good or bad?"

"Yes."

"And the good people are always good?"

"Absolutely."

"And the bad people are always bad."

"Yes indeedy."

She paused and appeared deep in thought.

"But can the bad people change?"

"Sometimes they do, but most of the time they stay bad."

"It seems so unfair," she said.

He was pleased to have diverted her attention so easily from the question of how she was "different."

He explored the moment.

"There are three kinds of people in the world," he told her. "The bad, who are generally bored. We call this *charisma*. Then there are the good, whose lives are frequently wracked by turmoil. We call that *character*. And then there's everybody else. We need the good and bad people–we try to get away from the bad ones and get near the good ones."

This one wasn't so bad, he thought, but he'd have to get away from her rather soon.

They had a late dinner downtown. They took a long walk along the harbor promenade, which still smelled faintly of spices and fuel oil even though the spice factory was now an office complex and the only big ships that still called were the destroyers and training ships of foreign navies.

They stood by the still water where the harbor lights hardly danced at all. It was a little like a TV commercial for a good whiskey or a bad perfume. While they watched the lights, jazz from the music pavilion drifted across the wide water.

A smiling man came up and asked if he could show them his war wound for a quarter, jerking up his pant leg and pointing at an arthritic knee.

"No thanks," Foote said.

"Today's muh birthday," he said proudly out of a toothless smokestack of a mouth. Foote nodded as the man veered off to intercept another strolling couple.

He was suddenly tired. And in a slow, gentle arc, he turned their path toward the parking lot. When he dropped her off, he told her it would be a while before he'd see her again, since he'd be out of town for while. Ed had convinced her that he was an engineering consultant for one of the big oil companies and was going on a perilous operation to the Arabian Peninsula the next day. She begged him to write. He promised he would.

In fact, Ed Foote was an ornithologist for the Baltimore City Zoo. He was in charge of the health and welfare of a variety of wonderful bird specimens, including the Painted Macaw, the Hollering Roo, and the Vice-billed Parrot, which was capable of crushing a man's hand with its beak if it got the chance.

But by far the most important part of Ed's job was closing the door on the cage of the Blue Bird of Happiness, once it returned to its roost after spending the day singing in the biggest oak tree in Druid Hill Park.

Every day the zoo was open, rain or shine, Ed was alongside the cage to carefully latch the big wrought iron door. The cage was more for keeping anyone or anything from getting at the Blue Bird of Happiness than for keeping the Bird captive. It had absolutely no desire to fly away. It would simply wait until Ed opened its cage door each morning and then fly to the big oak tree, where it sang a song people said could make strong men weep with joy.

In twenty years of working at the zoo, Ed had never missed letting the Blue Bird of Happiness out of its cage in the morning and greeting it each evening at dusk as it returned to its perch.

Officer Shoemaker, the rent-a-cop in the aviary building where Foote worked called him "Old Faithful," and wondered aloud frequently when Foote would one day call him to ask for his help with the Blue Bird of Happiness.

"Any time you need a day off, just give me a holla," Shoemaker would say.

"I will," Foote would tell him, "but I can't imagine ever missing my appointed rounds. But thanks for the offer, Norris."

Ed couldn't explain why but he never did go down to the park to listen to the song of the Blue Bird of Happiness, although most people who came through the birdhouse told him of its singing and how beautiful it was. Ed would just nod and smile and point to the big iron cage the zoo had built to keep people and animals away from the Blue Bird of Happiness while it slept.

"He's so happy all the time because he knows he'll sleep safely in there at quitting time," he'd say.

Foote relished the lore that had grown up around the Blue Bird of Happiness and its song. He thought the stories helped promote the zoo and the aviary. He also thought they helped ensure he'd continue to have a job. He'd tell visitors how some people would come to the zoo and hold their babies' baptisms and their birthday celebrations and their weddings in the shade of the big oak tree where the Blue Bird of Happiness sang all day.

"They come because they believe the song will bless their babies, and their birthdays, and their marriages," he'd tell the visitors. "It's not so far-fetched, actually, since it's a fabled song people say can make strong men weep with joy. Not a bad way to bless a marriage."

Ed himself had been through two bad marriages in those twenty years and didn't put much stock in weeping for anything, joyous or otherwise. He spent most of his time off either at the athletic club playing around with the free weights or at the Laundromat picking up married women or at the places in Fells Point where you could still toss peanut shells on the floor without getting thrown out.

The night after walking along the Harbor, meeting the bum with the war wound, he put on his old gray tweed sports coat to go out for a few drinks. He hadn't had the coat on in years and it fit him as if he had been boiled in it. When he unconsciously checked all the pockets, in the right inside breast he found a handkerchief with the crimson lipstick smear on it. That brought it all back, brought her back. He could see her: Daisy McQuillen.

He stood there, staring at the handkerchief and the lipstick mark, transfixed by the wave upon wave of memory emanating from it. It was as if he were hearing an old romantic tune. He took off the coat and made himself a scotch and soda. After studying the artifact for a few moments longer, he stood, as if the trance had ended, and went to the study. He rooted through one of the junky drawers in his desk, trying to find his old address book.

He hadn't seen Daisy in at least five years. He remembered the last time they were together at a party in Fells Point. That night she kissed him hard on the cheek and left the lipstick mark that he later wiped off. After that he didn't call her for a while and the next thing he heard was that she had moved to Annapolis with some architect and got engaged.

When her husband left her, not only for another woman but another coast, Daisy was heard to remark to her friends that she felt as if part of her had been taken away. And she knew it sounded cliché. But then one of her friends showed her an article that said scientists had made a startling discovery about relationships.

The scientists had found out that when two people lived together, they indeed actually began to share cells from each other's bodies in a variety ways, including kissing, sexual intercourse, using the same towels, bathtub, occasionally using the same utensils, cups, and dishes.

After a time, the average percent to which two people's bodies shared cells and were thus biologically joined was established at .079. This meant that for every one thousand cells in one partner's body, approximately seventy-nine of them came from the other partner's body.

This didn't make Daisy feel one bit better. It only served to underscore how awful she felt. Daisy told her friends that she didn't want to read any more articles, or go on any more weekend trips with strange men, or have them give out her phone number to men they thought she'd like. She wanted them to stop worrying about her and didn't want to talk about anything just yet.

Almost as if she were living a scene from a movie, the night she felt worst about her husband's walking out, she got a call from an old boyfriend, Ed Foote, the guy she remembered did bird calls and slept with his socks on.

They talked for about two hours before she broke down and told him about her marital problems, an expression Ed thought was redundant anyway. They talked until it was nearly morning, she marveling that fate had an old friend and sometimes lover call her; he thinking what a marvelous stroke of luck that she was on tenterhooks.

He felt vaguely like one of the bad people in the soaps but acknowledged when he hung up that it was the scotch causing it.

They met the next day for lunch at the zoo concession. She was off that week from her job as a media buyer at one of the city's blue chip ad agencies. Ed, of course, never took days off, busted up marriages or no, since he knew, or at least thought that the Blue Bird of Happiness needed him to open the cage in the morning and close it every evening. And that was, after a fashion, true, too.

They ate outside and then took a walk through the big game cages, Ed pointing out the neurotic black bears and the self-possessed giant sloth.

She didn't want to talk about her life from the time they split until the breakup of her marriage to Dean Foreman, an architect in Annapolis. She'd speak only about the short time since her husband had left. From her silence about the marriage, Ed took that the separation was indeed permanent in her mind at least. He tried to make her feel better by relating the saga of one of his own disintegrated marriages.

"The day Ruth and I split, the robins had built a nest in the hanging flowerpot on the front porch and four fledglings hatched. From the living room window you could see their downy wild feathers splaying in the breeze, and you applauded the ingenuity of the parents, for up there, hanging under the rain spout, no cat could climb and the gigantic bumble bees rooting through the azalea flowers below paid them no mind. The two worked hectically for days feeding the tireless mouths, which, day by day grew into fine strong robins themselves. The way they jostled and prodded each other, you wondered why one didn't fall out, but that never happened. You kept watching, thinking you could put one back or scare away a jay or marauding crow, but you knew that was impossible, and that nature, embodied in those sleek parent robins, looked at a fallen fledgling with cold glassy eyes. That is, I have come to imagine, the way Ruth and I began to regard each other, as piece by piece, our lives fell away from the marriage. We finally paid each other no mind."

Ed was shocked to see her gazing at him. He thought maybe he had laid it on too thick. He was pretty tired from having spent most of the previous night talking on the phone, but too interested to let her see it.

"That's sad," she said, "but I do understand how you felt. I mean my gut hasn't stopped hurting yet. I guess it all is, in a way, very biological, very–chemical."

"They say that in the beginning, God never intended man and woman to live together full-time," he said. "All along the two were supposed to live separately and only get together on the weekends."

She started to laugh, took his hand and squeezed it.

"But Satan, the wily old goat," he continued, "got men and women together by instituting rent and mortgage payments, which somehow led men and women to believe they were supposed to live together naturally. Part of the deal later on was that God was supposed to make men and women feel as if it was okay to be that way. This was curtains to any thoughts men had about weeknight poker games and women's fancies of playing Pilates videos in the living room. When God first heard about what Satan had done, he said, 'They'll be at each other's throats in under a week.'"

"So what happened next?" she asked.

"He took steps, of course. He invented lawyers."

She wouldn't stop laughing. He was happy he had made her so happy.

As they strolled by the cage of the male boar, the animal was nosing around in a pile of cornhusks. When Foote heard himself invite her to dinner, the boar casually looked up as she said yes.

At four thirty and she said she had to go move her car or it would be towed. He drove her to St. Paul Street and they found she had a dead battery. Foote was driving his beat-up Volvo so old that the trunk gasket had turned to tar and he to pry and pry until it popped open. His jumper cables were rusty and gnarled, but after a time they had Daisy's car going again.

They decided to have a drink in celebration of this achievement and Daisy took him to a little place she knew in Charles Village. She had a bloody mary while Ed had two martinis very quickly. So she parked her car at a meter and they piled into the old Volvo to go back to Foote's place for dinner. Ed, trying to remember the words to "On A Clear Day," showered while Daisy made an omelet. When they were sitting in the living room after dinner, she sat back and looked him up and down.

"This is the same way it was last time," she said. "You have me over for dinner, you pour drinks, you say—let me see, 'The world might just end tomorrow.'"

"I'm also particularly good sautéed in white wine and butter," he said not so much feeling his drinks as mischievous.

"You were very good at making me feel completely irresponsible, Ed," she said. She pulled her stocking feet up against her bottom on his sofa. "Why does it have to be so complicated all the time?"

"Was it complicated for us to break it off back then? Was it complicated for your husband to fly out to the coast without looking back? Was it complicated for my first wife to leave me one day with nothing but a spoon, a fork, a knife, and a roll of toilet paper?"

"It seems complicated. Breaking up with Dean made everything so complicated."

"Only momentarily. Pretty soon, the whole mess clears up like technical difficulties at the station during a broadcast of *Dr. Zhivago*. One minute he's the conscientious husband and father, the next he's thrashing around in the snow with Julie Christie. No problem."

"You're right," she said. "It *is* chemical."

Ed got up to change the music. "Birds know—birds, which are really lizards with wings, have adapted beautifully to all sorts of privation and developed wonderful behaviors for courting and reproduction. But the moment those fledglings drop out of the nest—bang! They act as if they've never seen each other before."

"But what about undying love and devotion?"

"If they help us survive, we'll keep them. If not—"

After they had another drink, like a forties movie detective from afar opening hand closing his wallet saying, "I am Joe Smith. Here are my credentials," Ed asked her to stay with him that night—and that nearly ruined it.

"I'm just not ready to jump right back into something. I really like you, but I have to give myself time. You know what they say about rebounding." She said all of this in one breath, shaking her head.

He was quiet for a long time. When his cuckoo clock sounded ten, he started doing birdcalls, which they both remembered used to make her helpless with laughter.

He stopped the birdcalls and kissed her. She wasn't that helpless, after all. And she wasn't not ready, either.

Ed Foote, ornithologist, aging raconteur, defiler of virgins and bane of marital fidelity, felt himself falling for her all over again. He held her and told her they needed to hear one more birdcall. He tried to imitate the Blue Bird of Happiness, but could only do a few notes before he broke off. She looked up at him and smiled.

"Not a bad way to bless a marriage," he said.

That night, as they curled around each other like swans, Ed had an anxious, disturbing dream.

"Swans are the only birds that mate for life," he was telling Daisy. They were in the zoo aviary building in darkness. They walked past the guard kiosk, where Officer Shoemaker sat at his post, sleeping soundly. They were walking to the big cage of the Blue Bird of Happiness, past the cages of the sleeping Painted Macaw, the Hollering Roo, and the Vice-billed Parrot. He expected to see the Blue Bird of Happiness on its perch, as always, having come back from a day's singing in the largest tree in Druid Hill Park. Its wing feathers would be puffed up around its head, keeping itself warm. He'd gingerly push the big cage door closed until he'd hear it latch…But as they got to the cage, Daisy put her hand to her mouth. The Blue Bird of Happiness was not there.

Ed awoke at daybreak and flew into a panic. He jumped into his clothes and fought his shoes onto the wrong feet. She sat up in bed, laughing and pointing.

"The cage! The cage!" He kept yelling it over and over, seeing visions of the lonesome Blue Bird of Happiness sitting awake all night in its drafty cage, the door open—someone or something trying to wring its neck.

He whirled in the bedroom, looking for his car keys. *A cat—a giant cat had gotten into the cage and eaten the Blue Bird of Happiness,* he said. *A maniac, a lunatic, a drunk, a bum with a war wound, a might have come in and wrung the neck of the Blue Bird of Happiness! After twenty years after twenty years—no more sitting in the big oak tree—no more song that can bless marriages and make strong men weep with joy—*

He stopped. She was laughing and pointing past him out the window to the flower box where, in its ridiculous teal and azure plumage, the Blue Bird of Happiness was perched, singing its heart out for Ed and Daisy.

Smart Boy

For JMC

I remember when all of this happened because of a fire. It was the night before the old wooden Oriole Park at Greenmount and 29th burned to the ground—when you could see the glow from all over town. Nobody knew what started the fire. Somebody said it was a thrown cigarette. Some people said it was the Krauts. Whoever did it they started checking people real careful after that. That's why I still think she didn't have long to wait before they got around to deporting her anyway.

She was the type you noticed as soon as she came into the room, and she knew it. A guy with my looks doesn't give her kind much of a second thought—at least not until she bumped up against me in Chauncey Rowley's crowded kitchen the night his latest play opened at the Illyrium. She was a dead ringer for—who was it? Myrna Loy: coifed copper-colored hair, skin like some kind of expensive porcelain dish, and that pouty rosebud mouth of hers.

It wasn't just one of those casual, social brushes, either. At first she pretended not to notice as she stood at the kitchen sink and dug through a veiny crockery basset hound jar for a match. She clutched the cigarette like she was going to shiv somebody with it.

I stood with my back to the wall and my hat tipped back like a guy just back from the trifecta at Pimlico with a losing ticket.

"Those things'll kill ya," I said.

She turned around and put the cigarette between her lips. So I lit it for her.

This one had at least some class because she didn't talk until she had taken it out of her mouth again. She had a very distinctive foreign accent I couldn't place and blew some of the smoke out through her nose onto me. Always such a charming trait in a woman.

"You are very gallant, Inspector."

"How'd you know I was a cop?"

"You were watching me."

"A guy looks at you, and he's a cop?"

"A lot of them look. You were watching."

"Cocktail parties do that to me. Pour you a drink, mademoiselle?"

I already knew what she was drinking. I reached for a bottle of it from a half dozen along the counter. You could tell it was the good stuff because the bottles had labels like European bank notes that said *Drink me.*

We had. They were all dead soldiers.

"Judge a wine by the label," my old man always said. That and twist the bottle not the cork. The old man knew what was what, all right. Funny thing about having it right, like that label, or that girl.

She said her name was Flora.

"You're a smart boy. Mind if I call you that, Smart Boy?"

She put her head back and inclined her white neck until I could see the smooth point of her Adam's apple. I figured she was about five nine, a hundred and twenty pounds. She was also probably half my age and looked like she badly wanted somebody to handle her. But I could tell something was up: nobody rubs up against a cop like that unless she's selling something. Or nutsy. Or maybe she just needs a policeman. She seemed frightened, so I figured it had to be number three.

"It's John Eben. You can call me Detective Eben," I said, scissoring two glasses of the bubbling stuff between four fingers of my good hand from a tray floating over everybody's heads on the palm of a kid in an oversized white dinner jacket.

"What time to we eat?" I asked the kid as he was sucked back into the crowd of bodies. He turned to answer, but then was gone amid the hubbub in the hallway.

When she noticed I hadn't taken my other hand of out my pocket, she poked me in the ribs and made a throaty laugh.

"We? Have a frog in your pocket, Smart Boy? Or is that your big detective pistol?"

The thought went through my mind of telling her about my go-around with three cargo hijackers on a dark wharf in Canton one night. I didn't think she'd want to hear all about bullet fragments and severed ganglia, so I shrugged.

"War wound."

Her eyes got big and she sipped on the glass I handed her.

"Did they give you the Purple Heart, Smart Boy?"

"Yeah, the Purple Heart. That's it."

"Do you like the champagne?" she asked.

"Not bad. That's Chauncey for you: shoot the moon."

"It is my family label."

I was reaching behind her to check the name on one of the bottles, when all of a sudden she was on me like a bum on a baloney sandwich. Right up on my neck and face with a tongue and mouth that tasted like too many cigarettes, tart and hot. When she had finished a good job of kissing me, she was already picking up her purse in a way that told me she had things to do and things to talk about.

"Tell you what, Smart Boy, take me out to dinner. My treat."

What did I have to lose? Besides, the party was getting way too crowded. Chauncey was reveling in his glory in the living room. A pair of twins, women dressed as Zouaves, sat cross-legged in an open dumbwaiter. You could already tell it was going to be a long night.

Now that he was famous, Chauncey Rowley had decided to simplify his life. He had heard that things get tough for famous people, but never really believed it until his play about D-Day, *Three Men, Screaming and Crying*, won the Pulitzer Prize and a National Critics' Circle Award in the same year. Chauncey wore old Irish cable-knit sweaters with holes in them, corduroys with smooth places and ancient boat shoes with laces that had turned to stone.

Flora and I beat it like scalded dogs and pointed a cab toward Mama Mia's. It had rained that evening and the streets were still wet. Then she started crying all at once and it all came out in between sobs like bad soap opera. I handed her my handkerchief.

"You are such a clean man," she said in that accent. I took it as a compliment.

"Thanks. My mother told me never leave the house without a pressed handkerchief."

"I will give it back to you."

"Keep it. My Aunt Wilma gives 'em to me by the dozen every Christmas."

"She is a good *Tante.*"

Before I knew what was happening, our driver slammed on the brakes and the door on her side flew open. Two men pulled Flora out.

"Now drive!" one of them yelled, slamming the door.

The driver began cursing in Spanish and floored it. The champagne had taken the edge off the day, I guess, and I was thrown back into the deep seat. I scrambled up to look back and saw Flora being shoved into a dark-colored sedan. I couldn't make the tags as we sped away from each other.

I called in an abduction, but couldn't run a check on Flora with no surname. Then I remembered the champagne at the party. Her family label, she had said. So I called Chauncey.

Somebody named Corinne answered and there was lots of music and laughter. The party was still going strong.

Chauncey was half in the bag. "You left with Flora Briand! My God, Eben, you're old enough to be her father."

"Why would anybody want to kidnap her?"

"Maybe her visa expired," Chauncey said and hung up.

I called in the make on Flora then I checked my service and got a message the Chief wanted to see me.

It was ten blocks uptown and that gave me a chance to collect my thoughts.

"Here's that make on your soubrette," said Miss Abernathy as I walked through the Chief's outer office. I quickly read the rap sheet. Nothing except that her papers were already expired—she was in the country illegally. I put a call in to my friend Pino Gallagher down at immigration. They had her locked up down at the Customs House and were shipping her back on the next flight to Lisbon out of Martin's airfield.

"What was she doing here, anyway?" I asked Gallagher.

"She says she was in the salvage business."

"Salvage?"

"Yep. We spotted her two weeks ago down at the warehouses looking over a shipment of crates. We almost grabbed her then. She disappeared. Had a wad of hundreds on her," Gallagher said. "You got anything?"

"Nothing. Do me a favor and keep her there until I can get there, okay?"

Gallagher said he'd try his best.

Briand. Briand. A quick check at the Pratt confirmed my suspicions. A story from *News American* dated May 12, '44 reported that a German submarine sank off the New Jersey coast in early spring that year with a cargo of French champagne aboard. The Germans were plundering stores in France and shipping the booty to Central America. The submarine broke its rudder and was blown off course by a storm and sank off the coast in the dark of night. Then I called my buddy Arthur down at the FBI for anything more recent involving Briand and a fortune in cases of champagne.

Nothing.

I went home to sleep but didn't because I kept thinking about Flora. The next morning, I showed up at Chauncey's apartment with about a dozen questions. It turned out that Chauncey knew the Briands pretty well.

I caught a cab down to the Customs House. It was near midnight and had started raining again.

They had her in an upstairs office, big picture window overlooking the city.

"What was so important in those crates that you had to risk arrest and deportation to find?"

"It was my grandfather's entire 1943 vintage. It was all they brought when they came to this county. Somebody gave his brother Vincenzo a box of Cracker Jack, and he was so thrilled, he ripped the top off and started to eat it. He choked on the Toy Surprise and died."

Funny thing about Toy Surprises, I thought, Life is full of 'em.

The immigration men put her in the car. I have to admit, I felt a little sorry for her. They let her roll down the window before they drove her off to put her on a plane back to Portugal, no doubt to spend the rest of her days as a label checker at some stinking Madeira bottling plant.

"I love you, Smart Boy," she said. "Please always remember me." And with that pouty mouth she planted a soft, wet kiss on my cheek.

I tell you what: I didn't wipe that one off for a long time.

Poke Supreme

When Cray mainframe and an eight-armed robot teamed up to take his job at the box printing plant away, Hector Thorpe made two decisions. First, he decided it was time to join a book club. He joined a good one, too: as his initial membership subscription, he got to pick 12 high quality paperbacks for just $1.79. Every selection after that was $7.95 plus shipping and handling charges, and he had to buy four more books in the next year or something awful would happen but Hector had learned by now that he'd better start crossing bridges when he came to them.

He unwrapped the 12 books on the morning they came and stood them up on the mantelpiece between two potted plants, a Wandering Jew, and its enemy, the Christmas Cactus. One of the books Thorpe had ordered was a new book put out by, of all places, Motown Records. It was a combination cookbook and guide to the latest hip-hop dance moves. It's name: *Whip it, Beat it, and Stir it up: A Funk Foods Guide.* (The book club Thorpe had joined had a sublime sense of humor.) He thought his girlfriend, Emily, would like the books, particularly the primer on shaking and baking. She did.

The other decision Thorpe made was to enroll in night school at the Game Show Institute of America. The Game Show Institute was near Thorpe's house in Washington D.C., which wasn't far from such places as The Mall, the Lincoln Memorial, and the 14th Street Bridge. A kind of Hogwarts for underachievers, the GSIA was the only officially certified school in the country that held regularly scheduled classes to instruct everyday studio audience members on how to become big money winners on any of the network game shows they wanted to. Some of the GSIA's alumni had gone one to win big on such shows as *Wheel of Fortune*, *Who Wants to be a Millionaire*, and of course everyone's favorite, *The Price is Right.* Thorpe himself had aspirations to one become champ on his favorite game show, *Jeopardy*. He liked that one best because he thought it took a lot of skill to think up the questions instead of just the answers as on other shows.

Emily didn't like *Jeopardy*. Emily was a lottery fanatic. She liked watching the little white balls bounce happily up the chute while the announcer crooned out the numbers between the evening news and the next installment of *Inside Edition*. She liked the clean, quick decision of it all; she hated having to think about anything very much.

"Lotteries are a tax on ignorance," Thorpe told her, thinking himself very smart for having enrolled in the Game Show Institute of America. Emily didn't disagree or get angry because she didn't understand what Hector was talking about. She loved him, though, and dreamed one day of hitting it big and taking him away from dead-end factory jobs.

When Thorpe got his schedule of courses, he called just about everyone he knew and told them, except his ex-wife, who only would have told him once again what an asshole she thought he was. He reflected that Lorraine wouldn't have like the Motown sip and dip guide, either. But that was all someone else's problem now. He envisioned his life as that big clackety-clack wheel on Wheel of Fortune, and thought it better that he and Lorraine were on opposite sides of it now.

Thorpe's courses all fell on Monday or Wednesday nights, and the school prospectus informed him that he needed to keep one day a month free for field work and research. His courses ranged from "Quick Response, Level 100" to the very cryptic sounding "Odds, Luck, and Statistics." The school wasn't cheap, either, but as the school's founder explained in the forward to the student manual, nothing in life came cheaply, especially big jackpots.

The afternoon of the day before his first class at the GSIA, Thorpe went out into his backyard and washed and waxed his car. He polished it until it shone like a new one on *The Price is Right*. Thorpe owned a 1966 Cadillac that sat out back with a trunk and rear fins like a rocket ship. He kept putting his textbooks into the big trunk and taking them out again, alternately thinking that he'd forget them or that they'd be stolen out of the car.

When he got home from school that night, Emily made a big dinner for him and read to him from the Motown cooking/dancing guide. As they sat eating, Thorpe too nervous to listen, she read a recipe for a salad called "Poke Supreme," that called for alfalfa sprouts.

"It says here 'Use alfalfa sprouts because they are earthy and potent and will energize your mojo.'"

Emily thought that reading from the guide might take Hector's mind off his classes. She knew how much the whole thing meant to him and didn't want him fretting about it.

"I've got to review Historical Trivia before tomorrow night," he said as they finished eating.

Thorpe had trouble falling asleep that night, kept thinking about his classes.

He had a mind like a birdcage: nothing stayed in save one bird and one song, yet it was open enough to admit the light and air of possibility, the illusion of the grand expanse of freedom.

When he finally fell asleep, he dreamt about a game show his subconscious invented called *Eat Your Heart Out,* on which contestants vied to avoid paying taxes on their winnings. The host was an IRS auditor who constantly haggled with the players. Thorpe didn't like the game; it was a game show contestant's nightmare.

After three weeks at the GSIA, the day came when Hector was to make his first fieldtrip. He found himself on a shuttle bus with about a dozen other GSIA students on their to a tour of the Smithsonian Institution, the GSIA's partner organization in disbursing information, trivial and bizarre. The organizer of the fieldtrip, Thorpe's professor in a course called "Natural and Historical Phenomena" was riding co-pilot next to the van's driver. Thorpe sat next to Ben Keeler, a 32-year-old computer programmer from Rockville. Ben Keeler was one of the only blacks in Thorpe's classes and was complaining that the professor was a racist.

"Here I am paying three hundred dollars a credit, and this motherfucker keeps asking me if I know who wrote *The Autobiography of Malcolm X.*"

"His mother did," Thorpe said, which Ben Keeler thought was pretty funny.

When they got to the Smithsonian, they went through the Museum of Natural History first, assembling next to the giant stuffed African elephant in the lobby.

"Married people live longer than single people," the professor said to the platoon of GSIA students around him. "Why?"

"Misery loves company," Thorpe muttered loud enough for Ben Keeler to hear as someone else answered the professor's question.

Stress, it turned out, was the correct answer.

"OK," the teacher said, "We're going through here very quickly, so keep up. Let's move it. Who knows how to quit smoking and lose weight at the same time?" He spoke without stopping, walking ahead.

"Cut off your hands," Ben Keeler said to Thorpe.

Several of their classmates looked suspiciously at the two men. Many people at the Game Show Institute were too serious, Thorpe and Ben Keeler agreed, and that was a shame.

When they had come to Seas of the World, a commotion developed just ahead of them. Thorpe heard a woman scream and people scattered in every direction. A man was standing about 20 feet away and held his overcoat open for all to see. What they could see, taped to his body in every conceivable manner, was enough dynamite to excavate for dinosaur bones right on the spot.

"All right, everybody into the whale," he yelled. "Hurry up or I'll blow this building into Rosalyn." The small crowd of people moved into the mouth of the plaster model of the great blue whale in the gallery ahead of them. It smelled of calcimine and mold in there.

"Hurry, or I'll trigger the explosion."

Thorpe and Ben Keeler looked at each other with disbelief.

"Hey buddy, just calm down now," Ben Keeler said.

"No talking," the terrorist yelled.

"What's this all about?" the professor asked him.

"Dynamite, explosions, bodies blown all over."

"What do you want?" one student asked the terrorist.

"I'm demanding that the government recognize me as an independent state. I want an embassy downtown and full diplomatic privileges."

"Wow," Thorpe said.

"We might be in for a stand off," Ben Keeler said.

Recognizing that the man was as jazzed up as bottled seltzer water, Hector Thorpe got an idea. The Game Show Institute of America really had improved his mind.

"How about if we tell you a joke. If you've never heard it, you let us all go. If you have, you can blow us all up," Thorpe told the terrorist.

"Wait a minute, now," the professor said.

"Tell it," the terrorist said.

Thorpe and Ben Keeler looked at each other.

"You have one?" Ben Keeler asked.

"Did you hear about the Mafia Godfather who decided to become a lawyer?" Thorpe asked.

The terrorist looked nervously from side to side. He shrugged. Thorpe delivered the punch line.

"He makes you an offer you can't understand."

"I've heard it!" the terrorist yelled.

He started to little push a button on a black box on his chest just as a National Parks Service sharpshooter poked his head into the mouth of the whale and Tasered the terrorist from twenty-five feet. The terrorist curled up in a ball on the floor of the whale and slept like baby.

Ben Keeler whacked Hector Thorpe on the back. "Righteous, my homeboy!"

"I hadn't heard it," the professor said, quietly.

"I'm not in Game Show School for nothing," Thorpe told the admiring crowd. "My old lady and I have a book of recipes you might like," he told Ben Keeler. "Ever heard of *Poke Supreme?*"

The two left the museum shaking hands over their heads, waving to the cheering throng.

Slow Motion

The first day at school was unusually clear and cool for late August. As Kip Roland opened his classroom for the first time, the door cracked away from the ancient varnish on the jam, and he was hit by a wave of eraser dust and old book glue. He walked to the tall windows and raised one of the manila-colored shades.

Most of the kids who attended St. Dunstan's came from wealthy families along Charles Street and mockingly called the place 'Stan's' for short. In his interview, the headmaster Dr. Galloway told Roland that St. Dunstan's was a co-ed high school that long ago had given up its Episcopal affiliation.

"That's OK," Roland told him, "I long ago gave up all my affiliations, too."

The teacher next door was preparing that room, and Roland wondered how they'd get along as neighbors. Then he heard the blare of a TV monitor.

The headmaster had warned him about the teachers who had fallen prey to using video in every class, the ones who taught *Moby Dick* by showing the movie, or science by showing back episodes of *Nova*. They wanted to curb the abusive, unaccompanied, video lesson. The tests for those courses, the headmaster said, were always multiple choice, no essay.

Roland unlocked his desk, threw his keys in the top drawer and walked out into the hall.

The teacher next door was an attractive woman Roland thought was in her early forties. She was setting up a TV and video deck in the front of the room. On her desk was a startling familiar object–a copy of the last present Roland had given his ex-wife Mallory. It was a big executive coffee mug depicting a woman in a business suit clutching her hands to her face. The caption said, "Oh my God! I forgot to have kids!"

Roland had meant it as a good-natured tease. Mallory left it in the cupboard when she moved her stuff out.

"Anything good on?" he asked.

The red-haired teacher straightened and without looking at him, began to wipe off the TV screen with a cloth.

"How about midget whipped-cream wrestling?" she said, still not looking at him.

"What's your subject?" he continued, going into her room a few feet.

"Fluid dynamics and the effects of turbulence on acceleration vectors. Got a problem with that?"

"I'm Kip Roland. American history. We're classroom neighbors."

"Welcome to my world," she said, waving at the lab.

Roland smiled. "They told me to stay away from TV."

"Galloway hasn't been in a classroom for twenty years. Want to try drawing a three dimensional model of the space-time continuum on a blackboard?"

"I guess it has its uses," Roland said, and turned to go out.

"You're that baseball pitcher, aren't you?"

He stopped in the doorway and took a breath. "Yeah. I played a little in the minors."

"You'd been picked up, hadn't you, before—"

Roland nodded.

He didn't want to talk much about throwing the last pitch of his career in Hagerstown one afternoon two years before that killed a man in the batters' box. Oates Stanton had been one of Roland's best friends all through school.

That had been some pitch, all right. He'd kicked high and uncorked a fastball that had caught old Oates square on his right temple. He was killed instantly, they said, by a massive brain hemorrhage. Roland hung up his cleats for good that day.

"You'll do all right. Remember, don't smile before Christmas."

"Thanks. What's your name?"

"Maggie—Maggie in physics."

"Thanks, Maggie." He went back to his room and with the long hooked pole started to open the windows.

Roland didn't smile that month or the next. He remembered from a philosophy course at Towson that educate means "to lead out" and so he started his eleventh graders in a discussion of a diagram he had carefully drawn on the board of Plato's "Cave" He told them how, bound in the darkness, the captives watched the shadows flickering on the cave wall.

"Like in a movie theater," one boy said loudly from the back. "Like in *The Matrix.*"

"So what's the difference between the people who stay bound up in the cave watching the shadows flicker and the one captive who is able to climb up the slope into the daylight?" he asked them. The class of bored juniors lolled in the September afternoon air. The bittersweet smell of the first damp leaves and last-cut grass wafted through the room.

A gym class was out on the practice field and several heads were turned, watching a huge large soccer ball go up and down across a sea of undulating arms.

A skinny girl in the front row corner—Roland still couldn't remember her name—was looking from him to the drawing and back.

Several of the others started stacking their books, rehearsing for the end of class. A husky football player crouched half in and half out of his seat.

Roland walked to the front of the football player's row.

"Carnegie?"

The big boy flopped back down in his chair with a loud sigh and looked up at the ceiling.

"Uh—some people stay home and watch TV and—uh, some people like to get out in the sun," he said. Several other boys snickered.

Roland looked at the cracked leather toe of one of his loafers. The tassels were akimbo and chalk-dusted. The beadle raised his hand and said "Time, Mr. Roland," quietly. It was the signal. The entire class got up and moved toward the door.

The girl in the corner gathered her books and stood, looking at his crude drawing of Plato's Cave on the board.

He though she might say something, but as the last of them filed out, laughing and jostling, she turned and followed.

He decided that being a teacher traced the same contours as being a baseball pitcher. It was lonely, for one thing. To be the prime mover, the one who works the ball around. The Zen, he thought, the exquisite focus on throwing a three-inch ball at ninety miles an hour at a square not much larger than a history textbook.

The zone hadn't been that small for the guy Roland beaned. Everybody watching immediately thought, "Uh-oh, he's gonna' be mad!" But in the next instant they realized the collapse had been too final, too complete. He was carried off the field already dead, his right anterior lobe pretty much shattered by the direct hit from the rifle arm of Kip Roland. The sabermetricians scratched their heads and made another column in their books that season.

Roland had his first cafeteria monitoring duty that afternoon.

The big room was only lightly filled, since it was late in the day and only small groups of students sat around tables, some reading, some talking quietly.

He walked to one of the open windows and listened. He could hear Jim Thornton, a colleague of his, an English teacher, giving a lecture on Shakespeare's green world comedies.

It was one of those sublime moments in a teacher's life: quiet, orderly, academic.

As he listened to Thornton lecture his class about appearance versus reality, he glanced around the cafeteria and caught the eyes of a half dozen juniors, sizing him up.

As a new teacher, he was a curiosity to the older kids.

He thought maybe one of them was telling a dirty joke. The rest were looking for the monitor's whereabouts. They all snickered, still watching him. The zany breakneck audacity of sixteen-year-olds, he thought. He sighed and looked back out the window, listening to the late afternoon autumn crickets and Shakespeare.

"Prick!"

One of them had yelled it loud enough to be heard throughout the big room. Roland slowly took a step backwards without meaning to.

He heard all at the same table snicker again. The laughter spread all through the big room, this time even the kids who had been studying joined in, watching Roland closely.

He turned to face the table of juniors. Roland thought of squeeze plays he had executed flawlessly.

He made sure that he spoke to no one in particular, deliberately avoiding accusing anyone. "Tell your friend he's a marked man," Roland said calmly, carefully to the entire group.

The pressure at the table became palpable. They were all ready to burst—either into laughter if the situation resolved itself, or into self-serving denial if it didn't. Roland counted, waited, let his eyes meet each of theirs.

Some of them began looking around the table, others looked down.

Finally, Bo Nelson, a boy Roland had seen in the Prefect of Discipline's office before blurted out, "I didn't do anything! I didn't do it!"

"See," Roland said to the others softly, indicating the boy who had spoken, "I told you." He turned and walked away from them.

The boy continued to protest. "I didn't! I didn't say anything!"

Roland heard one of the others say to him finally, "Shut up, Bo. He's got your number."

One November morning, Roland caught the same boy drawing beards on a school student government election poster in a stairwell. He gave the boy a teacher's detention, which meant he had to come to Roland's class-room and write a paragraph on the blackboard. At the end, he'd tell Nelson to erase the punishment and clean the boards.

Nelson was glib when Roland came into his homeroom after the last class of the day. Other teachers had warned Roland about his tactics; his trick was to try to turn the enemy into an ally. He was a stocky boy, already muscled and well beyond the gawky phase of being a teenager.

"You were a pretty good pitcher I hear," Nelson said, wrapping his arms around the desktop to tie his shoe.

"Let's get started, Bo," Roland said, handing him a piece of paper with the punishment written on it. "You can leave when you've finished and cleaned off my boards."

Nelson studied the paper and slowly, his brow histrionically crinkling, walked to the front board. Roland was stapling tests on a table in the back on the room.

"I heard you beaned some guy."

He pushed the stapler down so slowly he could feel the staple inject into the paper below and bend up on both ends. Roland ignored him, kept on stapling tests.

"They say you killed the guy." He started writing on board in an awk-ward, block-lettering.

Roland stapled the next three tests sharply and jostled the stack. "Yeah, Bo, so now you know what you're messing with. Get going."

"Just curious, Mr. Roland. What were you throwing?" Nelson stood at the board, smiling, chalk and eraser in hand.

"Get to work, Bo," Roland said and walked out of the room and down the hall to lock the tests up in the department closet.

The idea of teaching came to him at Stanton's funeral. Roland stared when he saw for the first time how deep a grave was. He talked to Mr. Freiburger, their high school social studies teacher at the funeral. Freiburger had been their most-admired teacher, a man who had chain-smoked in class and used one of his desk drawers as an ashtray. After talking to Mr. Freiburger, Roland decided he wanted to teach.

When he went to put the key into his homeroom door the next morning, he saw a huge yellow gobbet of spit hanging on the doorknob.

He looked up at the faces around him.

"I don't suppose anyone has a Kleenex handy?" he said. The quiet girl, Maria Graham, reached through the press and wiped the doorknob with the sleeve of her sweater. "He's so immature, Mr. Roland," another girl whispered behind him, confirming his presumption of Nelson's guilt.

About ten days before the semester break, Roland noticed that the quiet girl, Maria Graham was absent more and more. When she was in class, she looked forlorn and red-eyed. Roland had found out that the girl came from a big family, with parents who both traveled on business a lot.

Somehow he was not surprised when Maggie McConnell, the redheaded physics teacher told him that word was the girl was pregnant.

That came one Friday afternoon after he had just finished a lesson—or rather a long digression—about Roman architecture. He told the class that when a Roman arch was finished, they made the architect stand under the arch as the scaffolding was removed. In this way, he told them, the Romans ensured their arches would be the very best they could be. Can lasting art or anything good, he asked, come from human suffering? They flooded out into the cold hallway.

He locked his classroom door and as he passed Maggie's room, heard her admonishing a boy—it was Bo Nelson.

"Now get your books and crawl out of here!" Maggie growled at him.

"How ya doin', Mr. Rolex?" the boy said jauntily as he passed Roland in the doorway. Roland waited until he disappeared.

"The kid is the prince of darkness," Maggie said. She was sitting up on a stool behind the lab table that served as her desk. He hadn't told her that he was nursing a blossoming crush on her—did she know it yet?

"Bo and I have had our share of attitude adjustment this semester," Roland said.

Maggie shook her head as she gathered up her work.

"I have complained to Galloway, but that kid's got nine lives around here. Funny thing—his old man just inked a check for a new wrestling and weight room."

"Them with the gold makes the rules, huh?" Roland said.

"Yes, and you've got little Maria Graham in homeroom, don't you? She's withdrawing Monday. Nobody knows where she's going. Galloway won't talk," she said.

Roland helped her collect her papers. "I knew she was having trouble when one of her sisters came in on conference night. Do her parents know?"

"Yes, and what's more, the rumor making the rounds is that your friend Bo Nelson is the daddy."

"I wouldn't doubt it," Roland said. "Except that I don't think he's got the correct number of chromosomes to reproduce. If we only had some proof. I for one would go right to Galloway with it. Get that monster bounced out of here."

She zipped up her satchel. "You'll probably need to go to the Board for that," she said. "And that'll sign our walking papers with Galloway. They've had their fill of crusader teachers around here.

"But what if we had proof?" he said.

"Proof-schmoof. That kid's golden. He knows he can make life hell for everybody."

"Sounds like you could use a beer. What're you doing now?" he asked.

She seemed as natural with the invitation as if he had offered her a stick of gum.

"Can't today. I'm supposed to be over at the field house with a couple kids working on an independent study project on the trajectory dynamics of a lacrosse ball. They're making video of about a thousand goals with a high-def, infrared, slow-motion filter. Neat, huh?"

"Fascinating," Roland said, in mock astonishment. "Maybe I can talk you into that drink Monday afternoon?"

"Yeah, sure," she said, laughing, "You—and Bo Nelson."

Roland walked out of the classroom wing, checked his mailbox in the teachers' room, and stopped by the Headmaster's Office on his way out. As he walked into the office, Helen Lowery, Galloway's assistant, told him, "He's with someone, Mr. Roland. Can I leave him a message?"

"No, no message, Helen, thanks," Roland said.

Just then Galloway's door opened and he let a well-dressed businessman walk out. The two were laughing and Galloway clapped his hand on the other man's back.

"Thanks, Peter, thanks a lot," Galloway said to the man.

As the man passed Roland, the secretary smiled big and said, "Nice to see you again, Mr. Nelson."

"Kip? Something?" Galloway asked as he put his hand back on the doorknob of his office. Within, Roland could see the plush, clubby appointments, the green leather chairs and the mahogany. A banker's lamp sat on Galloway's desk, surrounded by brass testimonial paperweights and letter openers.

"No, Mr. Galloway." Roland felt his jaw go tight. "I guess it's nothing."

On Saturday morning, Roland got up late, went out for a run through Wyman Park, then went down into Charles Village for breakfast.

When he got back to his apartment, his cell phone was buzzing on the mantle.

"Where have you *been*? I've been calling and texting all morning," Maggie said.

Roland felt a twinge of desire.

"Been out. Left my phone home," he said, "What's up?"

"I've got your proof! At least I think I do. Can you come in today?"

"What—to school?"

"Look. You remember the video project my kids were doing yesterday? At lacrosse practice? They got the balls all right, and the stands, and the trees, and the sky, and their boyfriends and each other. But there's something else I think you should see."

She had the video clip all ready to go when he got there, the screen all shades of red and rippling.

"Looks like Dante's Inferno," Roland said as she fooled with the color controls.

"Remember, it's infrared, so it's a little hard to watch-—but look at this."

She hit the fast-forward. The digital camera had faithfully recorded lacrosse balls zipping into the goal net, then swung up into the sky, wheeled around wildly, then jerkily panned the stands nearby. In slow motion, several huge red faces loomed up and girls screamed, "Hello, Miss McConnell, he-he!" Then someone off camera yelled for quiet and the camera wheeled back to the practice on the lacrosse field.

"Did you *see* it?"

"See what?" Roland asked.

She cursed and restarted the clip.

"Watch," she said, hitting play. "There—up in the stands—*look*."

She fiddled with the color controls and compensated for the infrared filter. There were groups of kids in the stands, some of them apparently waiting for cheerleading practice to start.

Off to one side, stood a couple.

Roland felt the hair on the back of his neck go up.

Bo Nelson was standing next to Maria Graham. She was standing with her arm across her middle, her head down, obviously crying, shaking her head very slowly. He slowly took his hand from her shoulder and put his arms up in what was it? Wonder–or exasperation, then said something in one or two words, his head snapping toward her, and turned to walk slowly away, now shaking his head.

The camera swung away from the scene to the sky.

"That's enough for me!" Maggie said, punching the off button and taking the flash drive out of the computer. "I want him to deny her in front of Galloway and his father, and then we'll show them this."

"And then we'll get fired," Roland said.

"Fired—this your proof! It's scientific. Listen, I talked to Bert Kondracke, Nelson's football coach. Even *he's* been looking for a way to bounce this kid out. This'll make their eyes bug out."

"It's just a conversation. It won't solve anything," he said. "This all happened in my high school—the girl leaves school, has her baby and the parents take care of her. The father's never identified."

Maggie's face flushed red. "Look, Kip. You, I, and every other teacher in this school have been searching for a way to nail Nelson. We've got it right here–he knocked her up and now won't have anything to do with her."

Roland shrugged.

"God—his old man will have a stroke! And then Galloway will have to kick Nelson out. He's a goner. And if his old man has any guts, he'll put him in military school where he belongs. Why should *she* be the only one to have to withdraw? Can't you see the justice in going forward with this?"

Roland put his hands in his pockets.

"Expedience, yes. Gratification, Lord, yes. Justice, no. Who knows? I might not even be here myself next semester."

Maggie threw the flash drive on her lab table. It skidded toward Roland and stopped.

"Look, I'm getting too old for this. I've put in twenty-two years in the classroom, and I've seen just about everything. This—I am telling you— beats all."

She went to the windows and looked out. "Call it wanting to get a little even with Galloway, of wanting to repudiate old man Nelson's stake in this place. Call it wanting to vindicate that little girl—or call it what you want. You can't save them all, Kip, and God help us, some of them you don't even want to."

He looked past her out the big windows. The light in the branches seemed silver. Roland thought of that moment when, irrevocably, the season turns. In a single afternoon time stands still, and the light reflects something beyond nature, beyond our ability to see.

She turned around, her arms folded.

"Are you in?" The silver light came through her hair and, for an instant, he longed to tell her how he felt about her.

"Let's talk about it over dinner at Wargo's. My treat."

"You're all alike," she said. Picking up the drive and brushing past him out the door, she hissed softly, "Goddamned short-timers."

Monday after third period, Roland walked into his classroom and threw his satchel on the desk. Then, instead of going up two floors to the faculty lounge, he went into the boys' restroom next door.

As he looked up from washing his hands, he noticed, among the graffiti along the wall, a message in red felt pen: *What does M. G. do in her last period???"* it said in the strangely familiar block lettering. Underneath was written, in the same hand, *"Easy, she didn't have one."*

Roland felt himself begin to tense and grow hot. He threw water on his face and then tried to rub out the scrawl with the damp paper towels; it was written with indelible marker.

He moved out into the throng of kids changing classes and pushed through to Maggie McConnell's classroom. She wasn't there, so he wrote a quick note on her blackboard.

> *"Let's show the clip to Coach Kondracke ASAP.*
>
> *—K."*

When he came back to his own classroom after lunch, someone had written something on his blackboard in a tight, intense scrawl. He recognized Maggie's hand and smiled as he read the note.

> *"Formaldehyde, a common organic compound on earth, has been found in its gaseous state in the space between stars and indicates a high probability that life exists elsewhere in the universe. It is a deadly poison.*
>
> *Galloway's office at 3. Thank you!*
>
> *—MM"*

Roland walked along the rows of empty seats and began one by one raising the big manila shades, flooding his classroom with the long silver afternoon light. It was going to be a busy spring.

The Green Bacon Boy

I think I decided to become a psychiatrist the day my grandfather admitted to burning his own house down because he thought it was haunted. He said that to insurance company investigators for months after the fire, when they were still stalling on closing the case, suspecting, correctly, that Dander had lit the match. But they only knew the half of it.

There was a whole lot more going on in that old man's head than an insurance scam. It wasn't about the money at all. He claimed to be listening to hundred-year-old ghosts. He was seeing things. He was stalking the farm at night and rattling chains. He was like an Alzheimer's patient on acid. Our Damma was a wreck, too, because she couldn't manage him. Within a year, it killed her.

I was sixteen and a half and I lived with my parents and two sisters north of Fenwick Island on the Atlantic Ocean in an old house with a lot of rooms. Our house even had some secret rooms–closed off dumbwaiters and root cellars–even an old butler's pantry my dad found when he was restoring the dining room.

"Lots of places for ghosts to sleep," Maeve said, although there wasn't anything in the little closet when dad pulled the bookshelf down, except stale beach air.

I'm one half of a set of fraternal twins–you know, the kind that aren't exactly alike–the kind our uncle used to call "infernal twins," particularly when we misbehaved. And we did that a lot of that back then. My sister, Maeve is the other half. That's the other thing about fraternal twins: you can have one of each–a boy and a girl. She was not firstborn. She was second, smaller, darker, and she liked causing trouble early on. She's probably another reason I went into psychiatry.

My father, a man of infinite love but limited patience, would frequently and loudly suppose later, when we reached high school, that the two of us had split the gene God gave everybody for good sense.

Our mother good-naturedly answered by saying we had been conceived under a falling star up at a cabin at Dilahunt Lake, near the land her family first settled when they came over to the new world in the early 1700's.

My mother's brother, Uncle Dan, who lived with us in Baltimore as briefly as his wife had died suddenly, had a far more colorful imagination what with his Irishman's sensibility. He pronounced, winking at Maeve and me, that we were really changelings, fairy children, he said, left in place of normal, earthly infants. We wondered, in that case, where our real human counterparts had gone or been taken, and would we one day be turned out into the woods if the real children ever turned up.

Uncle Dan might have been yet another reason I became a shrink.

For her part, Mattie–short for Mathilde–the Austrian housekeeper my father afforded our mother for the first six years of our lives at our home in Govans, quietly said we were "of the Gypsies." She would utter this and could not be brought to say more. Maeve, for once I remember, was speech-less.

Marty and Maeve–we were both dark-haired and dark-eyed, impossibil-ity, our father the biology professor insisted, frequently. He and our mother, you see, in their youth were both blonde and blue-eyed. Such things simply could not be, he said.

Yet, here we were, mother said.

Our sister, Kerry more closely followed their pattern. She was red-haired and blue-eyed. But Kerry lacked Maeve's spark or my love for books and sports. Kerry was nine years older than we were and had graduated from college by the time we moved from Govans to our house here on Fenwick Island.

My father's family, the Truitts, were from Towson, and had made their fortune in the hardware business. Mother was descended, and that's a good way to put it Maeve says, from the Dilahunts of St. Mary's themselves—the old dark Irish clan who settled the gently rolling hills of central Maryland north of Baltimore in the 1730s and built the foundations of the town that bore that family name. Then, just after the Civil War, popular sentiment chiseled away everything of the old southern side of things and thus changed the name of the farm and its surrounding land from Dilahunt to Delhern. The family heritage became a label for what in later years became Delhern Estates, a tract of executive home sites that clear-cut practically every tree on the property.

Damma and Dander, our mother's parents—that's what we had called them, what Kerry had named them in baby talk when she was two—lived on the original Delhern Farm, the 400-acre horse and cattle-breeding farm near Butler in Baltimore County.

We visited Delhern on Thanksgiving and Christmas, and for two weeks every summer in August. Dander was somewhat obsessed with telling ghost stories, about zombies and headless Civil War riders and women in white dresses, and hired hands whose spirits inhabited the farm's pond.

That's how we first heard the story of the Green Bacon Boy. It's how Maeve and I discovered that Dander—our grandfather—might have been more than what he appeared to be to us—and more, in fact, than the whole family ever could have imagined.

On the outside, Dander was a farmer. On the inside, he was something of a romantic poet. A poet with a highly refined knack for telling hair-raising tales.

Damma had hand-made the pillows on our guests' beds, the beds our mother and her brother Dan had slept in, the beds that our great grandfather had hand-hewn from chestnut trees on the property in the days when Indians still roamed the place. He had finished them with varnishes and glues boiled down from horse and cowhides before they were sold to be tanned into stovepipe hats for the fine gentlemen of Baltimore. The pillows were huge down-filled affairs and Maeve called them "squishy pillows" explaining that they "marshmallowed up when you punched them on both ends, just so," she said.

In our bedroom at Delhern Farm—the bedroom our mother had slept in—was the lighthouse lamp Dander had bought from an antique shop owner along Howard Street in Baltimore, who said it came from the ruins of a failed lighthouse at a outpushing of land in the Chesapeake Bay known as Bloody Point.

Dander told us: "This was a place where, in the heyday of the oystering industry in the 1850s, dishonest skipjack captains would brain their day-labor crewmen, weight their bodies down with sash weights and bags of oyster shells, and dump them overboard in the one hundred foot depths, rather than pay them their day's wages. The legends of the sailors of Bloody Point are well known among the watermen of Southern Maryland."

The lamp was a cylinder of alternating brass and blown-glass rings that Dander had wired with an electric light in the 1930s. It gave off a dim, ghostly pale light that Maeve said was just what Dander had in mind. It had a single switch on a butterfly stem that made a click "loud enough to wake the dead off Bloody Point," Dander said.

As always, he had a macabre spin for this story as well. "If this light ever does shine overnight, it will bring up the crewmen from the dark waters off Bloody Point. They will come directly to it," Dander told us on more than one evening before tucking us in.

Every time it happened, I believed every word of it, but Maeve, my beautiful other, my different double, was fearless. She insisted that Dander just wanted to save on the electric bills. She suggested we leave the lamp on overnight and, upon waking the next morning, would point out to me how silly I'd been to have crept completely under my covers. This went on for some years in our childhood. I'm sure that whatever neurotic ticks I have as an adult trace their origins back to this.

Sometimes, Maeve would make me keep overnight vigil. And this I did not understand. If the zombie crewmen from Bloody Point were not coming anyway, why stay up and wait for them?

We'd lie in the creaky old beds until the rooster started crowing and we could hear the faraway song of the trains out in the countryside, talking softly by the light of the old lighthouse lamp in the room that smelled of the stale varnish and glue of the bed and the night table, the highboy and the dresser. To keep our minds off the sound of heavy, water-soaked zombie feet on the steps, we told each other we imagined we could still hear the whoop of the pre-Revolutionary Indians far off in Garrison Forest or along Falls Road heading into Baltimore.

On a still summer night Dander would begin again:

"In colonial times, even right here on Delhern Farm, people used to slaughter their own cows and pigs and put up the meats in smokehouses," Dander said. "It was a very hard job, but necessary to the survival of the farm and the surrounding community. Many times, farm families would gather together to do their butchering and smoking.

"My grandfather—Papa, we called him— built a smokehouse down by the crick, but after two seasons it flooded out, so a neighbor offered Papa the use of his smokehouse for a week to get the spring sausage and bacon put up. My father and I were helpers. It was a long process, smoking and everything had to be done just right. If you didn't leave the meat hanging long enough or if your smoke fires weren't tended just right, the meat wouldn't cure and it would turn green and rot. It was a day and night process, so somebody had to stay up all night outside the smokehouse to make sure everything was tended to correctly.

"Several days before we were to go up to start our smoke fires, there was a commotion on our neighbor's farm. It seems one of his farmhands had gotten into a terrible argument with one of his sons.

"The next day, the son mysteriously disappeared. The rumor was that the farmhand done away with the farmer's son, but nobody could prove this nor find the body. This all happened at the peak of our neighbor's smoking and much of his curing went bad. The day after that, the farmhand disappeared and so did one of the farmer's horses and two prize beef cows. The rumor mill had the farmhand responsible for the thefts, too.

"So here was our neighbor, kindly allowing us to use his smokehouse, yet he had a wagon load of green bacon. We felt terrible. He kept talking and talking about his vanished son and the farmhand— calling the missing worker "the green bacon boy" because the farmer said his disappearance had spoiled all the bacon and sausage. My Papa offered to smoke double that year and split with the neighbor.

"Finally, the farmer went thoroughly crazy with grief and burned down his barn, shot his cows, and set off in search of the farmhand to get his revenge.

"Papa had us set to smoking and my father and I took turns staying up all night at the smokehouse of the ruined farm, listening to the crying of the neighbor's wife and daughters in his absence.

"One night, I swore I saw a man walking just outside the firelight of where I sat all bundled up. I called to him and picked up my hatchet, because I thought that maybe the Green Bacon Boy might come back to get me. I kept hearing the sounds of chains rattling down in their well house, and that put the fright into me. But I hunkered down and didn't leave my post outside the smokehouse. All night I sat waiting, awake, thinking I'd never hear the rooster crow. When it did, I thought, 'I'm saved!'

"When I told my Pa and Papa about the man walking and the sounds of chains from the well, they told me that maybe it had been the Green Bacon Boy come back to avenge his murder—and maybe not.

"The crazy farmer never returned, nor was the son ever heard of again. Funny thing is before the wife and daughters sold off the farm their relatives came and filled in that well that well and pulled down the well house. Not a trace of it remains today. Folks still talk about the legend of the Green Bacon Boy and how he might still stalk the neighborhood.

"People hereabouts came to say that if you ever laid eyes on the Green Bacon Boy, you'd become just like him—a zombie, doomed to walk the night. After that night at the smokehouse, I still say I believe in him."

Dander's story kept us awake nights. But the old farmer in the story wasn't the only crazy one on the lot.

The fire thoroughly destroyed the house, and with even the chimney down, nothing was left standing. Damma was heartbroken. She died a week before the first anniversary of the big fire. Dander went of his rocker because the insurance company kept the property wrapped in yellow "caution: crime scene" tape for years, dragging their feet to settle the claim. They knew who burned the house. We finally had him locked up for good at Greenside Heights Assisted Living.

The Bloody Point lighthouse lamp was at Baugher's Repair Shop in Towson, being refitted with a socket and cord. It was all that survived the fire. Our father got a letter from Baugher's that no one had come to pick it up and they were wondering what to do with it.

We spent that one last night at our parents' house in Govans, waiting for the morning that would bring the ending of yet another of our family's households–and the beginning of a new one. Each of our bedrooms was full of boxes, so Maeve and I slept in Kerry's room in her twin beds. I locked my hands behind my head and studied the fluorescent foam stars and planets still stuck to the ceiling of Kerry's old room.

She was quiet for a long time.

"Marty, Dander said that if you ever actually saw the Green Bacon Boy, you'd turn into him. Well, Dander sat up at the smokehouse that night and did see the man by the firelight. But maybe it didn't happen that way. Maybe, after all, he did leave his post at the smokehouse. Maybe he did follow the sound of the chains into the well house and he did look down that well. Maybe he did find the body of that farmer's son. And maybe, what he saw surprised even Dander. Maybe the reason that farmer neighbor went crazy was that there were two bodies down in that well. The son's and the farmhand's. Maybe that farmer did catch up with the farmhand, after all. The farmer put him down the well where the farmhand had thrown the son's body. Dander saw them both. But he could never bring himself to tell a soul."

"Then he lied to that Papa and his Pa?" I asked.

"Well, to them, yes. But he did tell somebody about it, eventually."

My mind was racing. "Who?"

"Marty, he told *us*." Maeve was quiet again for a long time.

I lay in the dark and thought about the sailors off Bloody Point. I thought about Dander's telling of the smokehouse story.

"Good night, Marty. Sleep tight."

"Good night Maeve. Don't let the bedbugs bite," I said softly.

How could it make any difference now if the undead sailors of Bloody Point found us, I thought, if my own grandfather was a zombie? Had we put his story to rest because we knew his secret now? Was he free of his chains, at last and forever? Reaching up, Maeve turned on the one last tangible link to our past at Delhern, the old lighthouse lamp.

Its beam was to shine out to sea from our parents' house on Fenwick Island. I imagined its light traveled all the way out to Lewes, down to Ocean City and on down to Assateague. And that summer, I imagined I saw the light travel much farther, back inland, to Baltimore—and farther to the cold ashes by the filled-in well of Delhern Farm.

Its click was loud enough to wake the dead. Toward morning, when no one—when no thing—showed up, I fell asleep.

I've been a sound sleeper ever since.

Following Distance

It's Christmas time in the late 1950s. I am nine years old driving with my father, mother, brother, and sister into Pennsylvania somewhere. None of us talk because we think our parents' marriage is breaking up.

In 1950, the year I was born, hair was short and the fins on cars were long. The St. Louis Browns came to Baltimore and became the Orioles. In 1958, when I got my first coonskin cap and Davey Crockett jacket with the buckskin fringe, Johnny Unitas and the Colts won the Championship in the "greatest game ever played." My father had taken us—my brother, sister and me to the new Memorial Stadium that they called "World's Largest Outdoor Insane Asylum."

Mom grew up on a farm in Anne Arundel County where they grew strawberries and cantaloupes and green beans. When the war came, they converted to growing hemp and soy. She remembered going up the hill across from the store where the little shack sat. They'd take their cigarettes— not packs but saved whole ones they'd scavenged— to the spotting shed with the telephone. They didn't know one direction from the next, one engine from four, but they'd call the sightings in.

By the time my siblings and I had kids of our own, a thousand World War Two veterans were dying each day. Ours died when he was seventy-eight.

My twin brother Billy called with the news about our father.

"Daddy died in a minor car accident," he said. "Hardly any impact. The paramedics couldn't understand it from what witnesses said. There was no damage to the car or the bridge abutment. It wasn't enough of a collision to kill him. That's why they want to perform the autopsy."

I got the envelope in the mail two days later with my father's St. Christopher's medal enclosed.

Two months before this, sister Emily was calling.

"It's getting acute. He's drinking alone—a lot. He buys vodka buy the half gallon. It's getting out of hand. I think he's an alcoholic," she says.

Call the newspapers. Dad drinks.

I try to console her. "The people who buy it by the half gallon aren't the ones to worry about. It's the ones who buy miniatures to keep in the glove compartment you need to keep your eye on. They're drinking shots in secret because they don't want anyone to know, and that's even worse than drinking half gallons alone."

My father once said this sentence out loud: "God wanted men and women to get together and have babies, so he invented liquor." Quite the philosopher, huh?

He also served honorably, as I mentioned, in the Second World War. Last Thanksgiving, late in the day, after sixty years had passed, my father finally decides he wants to start talking about World War Two. Yipee.

My brother Billy, my older sister Emily, and I were raised Catholic, so of course our car had a St. Christopher's medal pinned to the visor, showing this big hulking guy carrying the Christ child through the raging waters.

There was some history to that particular medal, since it was the same one my grandmother pinned inside my father's Army uniform lapel when he shipped out of Baltimore from Fort Holabird in 1942 bound for New York and then England. It was supposed to invoke the protection of the Saint for my father in his journey to war and back. My mother made a solemn Novena to St. Jude at the Shrine downtown, begging the saint to somehow keep my father out the war. St. Jude came through—temporarily—and my father's ship had engine trouble of Newfoundland and turned back to New York. He was on a brand new transport two months later and didn't miss his date with destiny after all. (Funny thing about that holy medal: it was the only thing the Germans let my father keep when they took him prisoner in 1944.)

Back in the 1970s, ironically, the Catholic Church pulled a fast one and declared that certain saints weren't really historical people and took them off the list. That's how St. George the Dragonslayer and St. Christopher—among others—lost their sainthood. But some people continued to wear and display the medals even after that, almost superstitiously.

My father did. That's because he said that the St. Christopher's medal had worked for him in Europe. This was unusual, I now realize, for a trained psychologist, but, at the time, St. Christopher probably came in pretty handy.

"Once a saint, always a saint," my father used to say.

He was captured along with the rest of a U.S. Army regimental head-quarters medical staff during the German offensive in the Ardennes in late December of 1944, the last bid to throw the Allies back, the campaign known as "The Battle of the Bulge."

He remembered an air raid in late December and being taken into the basement of an old school, cold and dark, with about three dozen other GIs. The German guards scavenged some rope and improvised lamps by filling up spent 88mm shells with Allied axle grease. They got the Americans to sing Christmas carols, listening intently to the English versions of hymns they, too, knew by heart.

You couldn't stop him once he got going last Thanksgiving. It was almost as if a damn had burst somewhere in his memory, and his body and soul knew it was time for all of it to wash out.

"Captivity was tedium. One day a blur into the next. You couldn't keep track of the dates or days or months. But we all knew it was Christmas Eve when late one night two of our guards appeared with two GI helmets. One was filled with an awful, beautiful red wine and the other with broken sugar cookies they had scavenged from some bombed out bakery," my father said. "The Germans weren't saints," he said, "But they weren't all bad."

Just after that, the Allies broke the back of the big German advance and it was all over in less than five months.

Like a couple million other GIs, my father came back, finished his college degree in two years at Loyola College, got married, made three babies, and bought a house. By the time my brother, sister, and I were born during the early years of the Baby Boom, we had a "Woodie," a station wagon with wood-paneled sides and an analogue clock that never seemed to be able to keep the right time.

My father always insisted that he was an excellent driver. He knew, he said often, many tricks the professionals used. There must have been something to it because I never saw my mother behind the wheel—not once.

In the days before restraints and airbags, a careful driver like my father would reach out his arm out to hold the passenger back, as if the offer of a forearm was enough to stave off the violence of an accident. And he used hand signals: straight out for left, bent up at the elbow for right, bent down for stop. Following distances were a car length for every ten miles of speed. His laws for accelerating and braking: pretend there's an egg under the accelerator, a rock under the brake pedal.

When I was sixteen and not yet driving, he showed Billy and me a postwar used car catalogue.

"Pick one," he said.

He bought the one we picked. The car was in Florida: a 1937 Ford with manual brakes. He drove us to Florida to pick up the Ford, and Billy and I drove it, following him closely every mile of the trip back. That was our high school car.

As meticulous as he was about his driving, my father was also superstitious about things like roads that ran straight north and south. He believed—and sometimes bogusly demonstrated—that you could point the car up a northbound hill, take your hands off the wheel and let some mysterious force—magnetism or something he thought—pull you along.

I still have a knot on the back of my head from the time I hit the dashboard when my father stopped short to avoid hitting an Army vet with no legs who was blowing a trumpet in the middle Pratt Street. I had a scar on the back of my head and, like my father's war wound, I came think that it may always have been there. The doctor told my mother it was calcified bone. It came to symbolize for me both my father's intransigence and his love for us, a patience born of a kind of stubbornness.

Thanksgiving at our house, unlike at some of my high school friends' homes, was a reasonably happy place. Warm and wholesome, sweet smelling of mulled cider, pumpkin pies, and bowls of nuts and tangerines. "Courier and Ives," Billy would say every year.

Last year, this atmosphere, the presence of lots of company, and a couple scotches mysteriously got my father talking about his war experiences. The Battle of the Bulge, being taken prisoner at the headquarters, and being freed after Christmas in 1944.

His reminiscences covered a lot of ground.

"He's talking about the helmet full of sugar cookies again," Billy said to my mother in the kitchen, who was slicing a big ham with an electric carving knife.

"No, he isn't," Emily said. She was arranging deviled eggs on a big plat-ter. "This is something different this time."

Billy and I walked into the den. My father was sitting in his chair by the fireplace, hunched forward, talking to a whole bunch of our relatives who were sitting around him, listening.

"It was snowing heavily," he said. "I guess because I was an army cap-tain and I had had two years of college and had studied psychology, they sent me to talk to a young officer at a hospital in a little French town on the Cotentin Peninsula. It was late September 1944. We were well behind the lines, in a backwater of the invasion, actually, since the front had pressed on into France and Belgium toward Germany by then.

"'Humpty Dumpty" was the triage nick-name given by our unit's nurses to grievously wounded soldiers who couldn't be put together again—and who would certainly die. 'Jack Sprat,' on the other hand, were seriously wounded GIs who'd lost something—an arm, a leg, a hunk of their meat from somewhere, or they'd lost their minds, but who would probably survive.

"This young GI, a Jack Sprat, who wasn't much older than I was, twenty or so, insisted loudly that he was Jesus Christ," my father said. "It was not a common condition, but it wasn't unheard of, either. Shell shock—battle fatigue, they started calling it—is such a strange thing. Most guys just sort of folded up into themselves, like a cot. Standard operating procedure was to sit the boys down, give them a good talking to, and get them back up on the line as quickly as possible. You've all seen the movies, I'm sure. There was no time for the kid glove treatment. Right or wrong, there was *no time.*

"I was able to interview the young man twice before we bugged out for the front in Hurtigen Forest in early October. This young soldier described something he had witnessed—something horrible. Two German soldiers burned alive by phosphorus in an observation post near the village of Matin Sur Mer on D-plus-2. We thought at first that was what had put him over. But it wasn't.

"His unit's U.S. and the German artillery positions faced off with each other. But the tide of the invasion flowed around some German strong points, and the Allied commanders thought it more expedient to encircle them, move ahead, and mop up resistance later. Just what the Germans would do later on to us at places like Bastogne. That was the order of the day. At this one particular village our friend Jesus had come from, it became a kind of friendly game of chicken. The infantry had the Germans boxed in and they knew it. So our side set up artillery around the village and waited for orders. At the young man's post, they got to know the enemy battery's crew, their counterparts on the German side. They might not even have been Germans, but Czech or Polish or Russian conscripts. Hell, they even found Mongols at Normandy in Wehrmacht uniforms.

"The mopping up continued. In the pocket, the enemy probably thought they were going to get the chance to surrender and then get shipped to Canada, or, if they were lucky, the farmlands of Wisconsin or Minnesota.

"One afternoon our Jesus boy's unit received the order: destroy all pockets of resistance. They were told to zero in on the Germans, which of course by now was simple, since they had had so much time to pre-sight the enemy positions. Prior to this the propaganda officers were just firing packets of leaflets back and forth.

"So Jesus gets the order to shell the opposing artillery position with high explosives, dead on. The German artillerymen probably at first thought that it had been a horrible mistake. Poor sons of bitches probably all died thinking that.

"Our Jesus hadn't been the guy who fired the rounds. He had been the officer who had to give the order. It was too much for him. It was too much for a lot of us.

"It's a hard thing for most people to understand—what an accurate artillery barrage can do to human beings. There are lots of pieces of people. And in some cases, in direct hits, there's nothing but a cloud of red mist. The term is 'aerosolized.' Well, that's what our Jesus boy's unit did to those Germans. He said that the last thing they heard over the radio was a German artillery officer pleading with them in broken English."

I had to go in and help my mother out with carving the turkey.

Billy came around the corner and looked into the kitchen.

"Why is Dad crying?"

We walked to the door of the den and saw my father with relatives sitting all around him listening, in his chair, sitting straight back, head erect, tears streaming down his face.

It's Christmas time in the late 1950s. I am nine years old driving with my father, mother, brother, and sister into Pennsylvania somewhere. None of us talk because we think our parents' marriage is breaking up.

We see a row of little altars by the roadside. We stop to read the sign. A school bus accident. A bunch of little kids killed. My mother cries quietly. What a tragedy, she says. Not a tragedy, my father says, a disaster. Interesting distinction.

I'm holding my father's World War Two St. Christopher's medal in my hands. I'm holding the medal hoping that it will protect all of us from danger and thinking that you can't get life to play out at any speed other than its own, that when St. Christopher steps aside and death comes, the best you can hope for is that it's head-on, in an instant. Or maybe you get aerosolized.

Still.

White Asparagus

1.

What makes a man want to kill his wife?

Infidelity, in either direction, will probably do. Better, perhaps, than mere extreme disaffection. Husbands kill their wives out of madness, rage, dipsomania, boredom, and a dozen other conditions. But can it ever be a simple case of *dis*passion? Could a husband ever kill his wife out of sheer indifference? Ever the student of the workings of the human mind, I got the perfect opportunity to find out just as I was starting out in my career.

Insanity, my graduate advisor Dr. Cobb had told me on more than one occasion, is practically undetectable from a distance.

"Danny, you have to get close to crazy to really see it," he says. "And you have to embrace crazy to truly understand it." Cobb himself was a dipso-maniac and a loony, of course. But I never completely understood what he meant about proximity to crazy until I had what you might call intimate dealings with a couple who lived in our neighborhood, Doctor and Mrs. Charles Delaney.

And I will tell you her given name because she deserves that: *Lydia Garrett.*

In the summer before I was supposed to begin my graduate teaching fellowship in psychology at the Johns Hopkins University in Baltimore, my father died of an intra-axial hemorrhage—a sudden massive stroke—and left us—my brother Arthur, my sister Margaret, and me—with a family hardware business in receivership that none of us wanted. Our mother had died three years before in an acute-care nursing home he could by that time barely afford. We found out from the family attorney that we had to sell our parents' house in Roland Park to settle their debts; so, in addition to having to deal with an old neighborhood hardware store going bust, there was that to attend to.

His funeral was small, modest, and Catholic—a lot like my father and the rest of his family. He wanted cremation, so we obliged and kept his ashes in a box on a shelf in the cramped little office in the back of the cramped little store on Hillhurst Road in Roland Park. (Why one of us didn't take him home we still talk about at length.)

We also had to liquidate the stock in the store, and then try to get out of a long-term lease my father had held with an ancient north Baltimore development corporation for more than forty years.

It wasn't as if he was an outright failure: decades of his selling wallpaper and grass seed and plumbing parts to some of the wealthiest people in town put Artie, Meg, and me through some of the best schools in north Baltimore.

But by the time we were each old enough to break it to my father that none of us had any interest in the hardware business, the bottom had fallen out of the small neighborhood trade, owing to the rise of the big warehouse superstores with price guarantees that ring the city in every direction.

And which of these realities broke his heart? We could never quite tell. Oh, the good old customers who still lived in the big rambling Victorians in Guildford and Homeland and Roland Park still came to my father's store for their bags of driveway salt and their coils of hoses and their packets of flashlight batteries. But the walk-in trade began to decline just when they did.

And of course my father never advertised. That's the other thing. Never had to in the old days. And how ironic that—when a well-timed ad or two in the neighborhood newspaper might have alerted the young professionals buying into the area as the older folks died off or moved away that there was a small, but thoroughly stocked hardware store just down the block—he was gone. He just never got around to doing it.

2.

The first ad we ever run for Hillhurst Hardware is one that announces the going-out-of-business sale.

By default, much of this falls into my lap. Meg is teaching at History at

Stanford and Artie has moved away to the Outer Banks to run a kite shop in Duck. Me, I come back to Baltimore after college, and as the executor of my father's estate, find that the duty of tending to the house and the store falls to me, not so much by choice as by a kind of twisted up primogeniture.

I first encounter one of the old neighborhood regulars, Mr. Obst, when I am about seven or eight and start spending part of every Saturday at the store, helping my father bag up tulip bulbs or sharpen lawnmower blades on the big grinding wheel he has installed on the counter in the back.

Obst is ubiquitous: he is the neighborhood gossip, historian, archivist, raconteur—and voyeur who seems to know a little about everybody and everything that goes on. He is French-German, rodent-like in his nervousness, with a voice like a rat-tail file raking over a tin can.

"I luff gardnik," he regularly announces in the store to no one in particular.

"What do you grow, Mr. Obst?" I ask him.

"My favorite iss radishes."

My father hears us and laughs. "Growing radishes isn't gardening—it's a stunt."

"Naaaay," Obst growls.

A first-generation American whose children are all grown and moved away, Obst knows all about growing most anything you can find in a typical garden. My father seems to tolerate Obst's eccentricities and nosiness, since on most Saturdays he is too busy helping people with floor sanders and toilet snakes to answer questions about how to force an amaryllis or when to mulch rosebushes. Obst, on the other hand, has all the answers for the customers my father gently refers to him. He probably should be drawing a paycheck.

After my father's passing, I think Obst will stop hanging out at the store, but he doesn't. And I am glad of it. I can use the help.

Apart from my Alsatian volunteer, I inherit one official part-time employee, Birdie Sook, who's an interior design major at the Maryland Institute

College of Art. Tiny and blond, a bit of a tomboy, she always wears jeans and work boots and flannel shirts she never tucks in. I never tell her, but I develop a huge crush on Birdie starting from the minute I see her. Birdie runs Hillhurst's paint and wallpaper department—actually just one wide aisle of the store against the north wall.

Another fixture around the place is Gil Tennenburg, a forty-something factory sales rep who smokes Marlboros out on the patio in front of the store every Saturday and helps us sell, among other things, "Deco Doors," a laminate coating you can get installed over your kitchen cabinets that, along with some new hardware, makes your kitchen look "Deco-licious." Throughout the late 60s and most of the 70s, Deco Doors made my father a lot of money. Gil Tennenburg still does pretty well on them, too, what with retro décor having come back big. Tennenburg always says that he's expecting Formstone to make a big comeback, too, any day now.

"You ought'a be ready to jump on *that* bus," he says, forgetting for a moment that I'm trying to close the store down, sooner or later, not expand our inventory.

In truth, I am not a very talented retail hardware mogul. For one thing, I tend to give little stuff away—inexpensive stuff—and Birdie scolds me for it.

Whenever anyone has a complicated question, I find it easiest to recommend using a blowtorch on the problem. I start doing this when Dr. Delaney, another one of the old neighborhood regulars, comes in one frigid afternoon to report the water is off in his house.

Gil Tennenburg, who's tweaking the laminate samples on Deco Doors display, says it's probably a frozen water meter.

"Happened to me in the big freeze of '96. The meter is out next to the street under that round metal cover. City won't come near it 'cause even though it's on the other side of the sidewalk, it's technically still on your property," he says.

"What do I do about it?" Dr. Delaney asks, seeming quite demanding.

Nobody really knows much about the Delaneys, who move into Roland Park four years before my father's death. People see Mrs. Delaney going from her car to the house with groceries and occasionally digging up tulip bulbs along their fence line. She's an attractive, tall woman with snow-white hair and the once or twice I see her in Garrity's Market. I'm reminded of Katherine Hepburn's bearing and poise—and her fragility. She smiles at people politely and doesn't speak much. Obst has told us that Dr. Delaney works as an anesthesiologist at Union Memorial Hospital and he would know: Obst lives directly next door to the Delaneys on Oakhurst Road, two blocks from the store. Dr. Delaney's a tall and rangy man in his late sixties, well-dressed and lightly tanned, even at this time of year. He comes off as a little imperious. A ski bum by avocation? Caribbean vacations over the holidays?

Tennenburg shrugs. "I dunno, Doc. Try lowering a hairdryer into the hole?"

"I would need at least three hundred feet of extension cord," he says, dismissively.

"We can do that," I tell Delaney, who's eyeing up an end cap of one aisle filled with electrical supplies. After some discussion, Obst calculates that the extension cord option is too expensive for a one-time use.

I put my hand on a shelf and look at what it touches. "What about heating the meter up with a blowtorch?" I say.

Delaney, who's clearly irritated, claps his hands.

What am I, his dog? I sell him a TorchOmatic T270 Propane Torch Kit for $16.99 plus tax.

We hear through the grapevine a couple days later that Obst and the other neighbors see Dr. Delaney out on the median strip late at night, waving a lit blowtorch around in the meter pit. Delaney's distant superciliousness has made him no friends in the neighborhood.

3.

Late that winter, Mr. Obst is on a new kick. And when that happens, there's no stopping him; it's all he talks about. So this time, he wants to grow white asparagus. He's Alsatian, it makes sense, Birdie Sook says. She's read that they grow it in Europe a lot—particularly the French and Germans. Obst says it reminds him of his childhood in Strasbourg, when his family grew it in cut-in-half fifty-gallon drums after the war to sell to the restaurants. The subject becomes a new point of discussion for everybody in the neighborhood who comes anywhere near the store.

"Most important," Obst says, "you haff to keep te bed bankt up, to blanch tem." It was first grown in the West by the ancient Greeks and Romans, he tells us, who used it as both food and medicine. Obst thumbs through a gardening catalogue and shows everyone the different rootstocks available by mail order.

"White asparagus iss callt *spargel*, and iss less bitter tan te green plant." He reads to us from the catalogue and from books he finds up at the Roland Park branch of the Pratt. "Stock iss planted in colt wetter. Te first shoots callt *sprue* come up in te first warm dayss off spring," Obst reads. Asparagus, it turns out, is a good source of folic acid, a critical nutrient for pregnant women in preventing neural tube defects in newborns.

Birdie Sook is stacking wallpaper books and comes around the aisle to where I am helping a customer load patio pavers onto a hand truck. "Ooooh, I've heard about that," she tells us. "They say if pregnant women in poor countries only got enough folic acid in their diets, it would drastically cut the incidence of cleft palate worldwide. PBS did a special on it."

Birdie, Birdie, Birdie. If she only knew how much she is always on my mind, even when I'm pushing the hand truck up and down the hilly streets of Roland Park, making deliveries for people's spring yard work.

One day, I am coming back to the store from a delivery on Oakhurst

Road and pass the Delaneys' house. I am whistling and don't know what or why. I'm shaken out of my reverie about Birdie Sook by a surprising sight.

I stop whistling.

Some men with a big truck are unloading a hospital bed through the wide front door. I guess this makes sense, I think: Obst has mentioned that Mrs. Delaney is ill.

But a hospital bed?

As I pass Obst's house next door, I figure he has already planted his crop of white asparagus. He's mounded up earth in wide rows along the side of his house in a part of the yard shadowed by the hedge of trees that separates his property from the Delaneys'. I smell the heavy perfume of damp turned earth and peat moss and manure and realize spring is not that far off.

4.

That Saturday, Dr. Delaney comes in wearing jeans and moccasins and a beat-up Georgetown sweatshirt and buys screening by the roll. After hearing about his project to replace a basement door screen, I try again to be helpful, sell him some spline and a spline tool. He barely says thank you.

Obst, ever-present, hovering near the racks and racks of seed packets and flower bulbs, offers his advice.

"Remember to remoof te door from its hengiss. Place it on smoot grount wiz a blanket underneet. Udderwise, you will haff difficulty."

Dr. Delaney mutters something to him. Before he leaves, he asks Birdie Sook how to paint to cover stains. His tone is blunt and impatient.

"What kind of stains," we hear Birdie ask him in the paint and wallpaper aisle.

"Water stains. Mildew. Rust," he says without explanation.

Birdie pulls a can of heavy-duty acrylic primer off the shelf. The white can has the name in big red letters.

"This is the best," she says.

"I'll take two cans of that," Dr. Delaney says. "What the strongest acid you carry?"

Birdie is silent for a moment. "What do you need it for?"

"Household cleaning, descaling a basement wall, stains, those sorts of things."

I am in the middle of selling old Mrs. Porterhouse a TorchOmatic T270 Propane Torch Kit to burn the moss off her front brick walkway. I try to hear what Delaney is saying to Birdie in lower register tones. Obst is frozen like a statue, arranging seed packets on the upper shelf of the rack.

Delaney completes his purchase and asks that the cans of sealer-primer be delivered along with his other items. When he leaves, both Obst and I turn the corner into Paint.

"He wanted the strongest acid available," Birdie Sook says. "So I sold him a gallon of muriatic. That ought to do the job."

"Spirits of salt," Obst whispers in awe.

"It's hydrochloric acid," I say, picking up and reading the label of a gallon jug of the stuff. "What in the world is he doing down there?"

Two afternoons later, Dr. Delaney comes in and starts asking about the relative capabilities and models of a heavy-duty leaf chippers.

After he leaves, Mr. Obst is still looking out the door after Dr. Delaney.

"I hert dem arguing," he mutters softly.

Nobody's seen Mrs. Delaney for several weeks, so the thought passes through all of our minds: Sealer-primer. Muriatic acid. Chipper. Birdie Sook says that he's probably going to grind his wife up and bury her in the garden.

"He's attended at hundreds of surgeries, you know," Gil Tennenburg says, sipping a tall mocha java in the office. "He'd know right where to make all the cuts."

5.

Just after lunch the next day, when Birdie Sook comes in to start her shift, her eyes and nose are red.

"Have you been crying?" I ask her, though it's clear she has.

She says she went to Washington that day on a gallery visit with one of her classes to see an exhibit of work by the Dutch painter Johannes Vermeer.

"This guy, this really old guy, he was in front of everyone else," she says. "He was standing too close, right up against one of the paintings. The guard asked him to step back. We *all* asked him. Next thing, he's squirting something all over the painting! Right there in the gallery in front of us. The guards swarmed him and used mace—they must have gotten us, too, I guess," she sniffs. "They took him out in handcuffs. Thought he was gonna keel over right then and there." Birdie pulls her hair back into a knot. She is still partly wheezing from the mace and partly crying.

"Why'd he do it?" Gill Tennenburg asks her.

"Motive iss not important. Tey caught him. Tat's te important ting," Obst says.

"I just started crying and crying," Birdie Sook says. "The man was an old Dutch Jew, a Holocaust survivor. He kept repeating that Vermeer was a Nazi. Have you ever heard anything so crazy?"

"Vemeer vass no Nazi," Obst laughs, shaking his head. *"'Einer spinnt immer…wenn zwei spinnen, wird's schlimmer.'"*

None of us speak German, so we all look at Obst.

"'Someone iss always crazy…when two are, it's worz.'"

The painting the man sprayed with a strong household acid is "The Music Lesson," Birdie says.

"They said it can be saved," she says, wiping her eyes, crying and laughing at the same time.

6.

Still obsessing about his coming spring crop of white asparagus, Mr. Obst is explaining to a brace of customers who want nothing more than to buy a new snow shovel all about the phenomenon known as "asparagus urine."

"A majority off people produce the odor after eating asparaguz," he tells them as they sidle up to the cash register for protection, "but, statistically, only about twenty perzent of humans can actually smell it."

"Way TMI," Birdie Sook tells him.

I load Dr. Delaney's order of paint and muriatic acid onto the hand truck. I start up Oakhurst Road with the delivery and notice that, even in the bright afternoon sun, Obst's yard is in full shade—walled in by thick Leyland cypresses. I can see his asparagus mounds, raised, like graves and—for a second—I catch myself wondering what Dr. and Mrs. Delaney must think of what looks like an orderly Alsatian graveyard right outside their dining room bay window.

I carry the box of paint cans down the Delaneys' basement steps and find the basement airy way door open. The walls of the airy way are covered in a green mold. Maybe he did need the acid for this after all. I go in and notice the basement is dark and smells of a hundred things—dank corners and coal oil, paint thinner and laundry detergent, camphor and must.

I put the box down on a table by two huge old sanitary tubs. Then I see it. A brown wooden casement as big and as deep as a mantelpiece on the wall near the staircase leading to the first floor—first of four in the house above this. The box has articulated pocket doors outside and a set of sliding panel doors inside. As I slide the inner doors back, I realize I'm looking at— looking into—an old dumbwaiter. The ingenuity of Victorian builders never ceases to amaze, as Obst always says. I find myself chuckling at the uses this appliance must have seen in the hundred-year history of this old place back when there were servants around. Bringing laundry down, hoisting groceries up. Plates of food and splits of wine levitated from the summer kitchen to the butler's pantry during the lavish dinner parties along the way.

The dumbwaiter is as big as a small closet. Without thinking, I climb into the cabinet and pull the inner cabinet doors closed. The space is cramped and smells of old wood, varnish, and must. I notice on the inside a set of oiled chains.

"OK. Let's get crazy," I whisper as I tug one and nothing happens. I grab the other and pull hard and suddenly, silently, I am moving up inside the shaft of the thing, inside the walls of the Delaney house.

"Motive iss not important. Tey caught him. Tat's te important ting," I hear Obst saying as I imagine them hauling me out of the Delaney house later in hand-cuffs. "It was a special delivery," I'll explain.

As I move soundlessly up through the dumbwaiter shaft, I can see through the crack in the doors that I am passing the kitchen. Another few feet and then comes what looks like a first-floor landing. Then I am three floors up in the house, looking into a small sitting room at the top of the stairs. I quietly open the inner doors a half-inch and can clearly see directly into the bedroom opposite the sitting room.

Mrs. Delaney lies in the hospital bed in the darkened room. She's white, wraithlike, and no longer reminds me of Katherine Hepburn, but of my grandmother before she died in hospice. The formerly tall and athletic, almost lanky woman now looks as small and as colorless as a doll.

I can see Dr. Delaney walking around in the room.

"Charles." I can hear her calling to him in a tiny voice. *"Charles."*

He does not respond to her or even appear to notice her.

She keeps calling his name weakly and he walks right past her in bed. Finally, I see Dr. Delaney leave the bedroom. He has pulled on an overcoat and has car keys in his hand.

"You sad, crazy bastard," I'm thinking. "All that money, and you keep her cooped up I the dark? And not even so much as a 'Goodbye, you bitch'?"

When I hear the motor of his car turn over and catch in the driveway, I slowly open the doors of the dumbwaiter and climb out into the sitting room at the top of the stairs. The house is silent, except for a ticking clock downstairs and the soft hiss of the steam in the radiators. I take a step and the floor creaks.

"Charles." I hear her small and far away voice again.

I slowly walk into the bedroom and then suddenly see the familiar oxygen tank, the IV drip, the clipboard hanging at the foot of the bed. I've seen end-of-life care firsthand before, and her chart records the schedule of a night nurse. *Lydia Garrett Delaney*, says the name on the chart.

I go to the big windows and throw back the drapes. The room is bathed in the afternoon light.

I look at her and her eyes follow me. Her face is calm, relaxed. There is no alarm, not even question.

"Lydia," I say quietly.

"Your name?"

"Danny." I tell her. "In hardware."

She half smiles and nods, recognizing my face from our few chance waves along the block and at the grocery.

I go out into the sitting room and bring back a chair. I sit by the bed and hold her hand.

All we can hear is the ticking clock and the radiators.

When the clock—a big old grandfather from the sounds—plays a metallic tune and clangs two, Mrs. Delaney looks at me with distant, mischievous eyes.

"I would like to have a piece of chocolate."

7.

The dumbwaiter is the quickest way I know into the basement and out the back. The driveway is still empty and I think how amazing he leaves her alone so long. I walk down the hill to Garrity's Market on Roland Avenue and buy bar of chocolate—that Swiss kind with the honey and almonds in it. A little expensive, but heck—last requests this simple don't come along every day.

When I get back up there, she appears to be sleeping, but stirs when she hears the floor creak again.

So I hold Mrs. Delaney's frail, white hand for what seems like another hour, feeling her grip, which is cool and firm. Her white old face grows placid as she lets the chocolate first warm, then liquefy in her mouth.

The house is still as the afternoon sunlight streams in the windows on the south side of the house. It will soon be spring and the business—ironically for me—will start to pick up as people—the old regulars as well as the newcomers— come in for their boxes of grass seed, coils of hose, and bags of cowshit.

I look at Mrs. Delaney's face and see a lifetime of worry and care—and what else is there?—begin to melt away. From the corner of her mouth a droplet of the rich chocolate dribbles slowly. Her breathing shallows. Then it stops. Her grip on my hand grows firmer, colder.

What will he think when he comes home to find her? Will he stare at her chart and clinically try to figure out the true cause of death? I straighten the bedclothes and smooth her hair back from her cool forehead. I smile as I think that he'll never figure out how she got one last taste of this sweet earth.

I skip the return trip in the dumbwaiter this time and slowly walk out of her bedroom, through the sitting room and down the darkly paneled staircase, and slowly descend past the coffin corners at each landing. The house is quiet except for the insect-like ticking of the grandfather clock in the front hallway. I go out the big leaded-glass front door and carefully let it click closed behind me.

8.

One warm spring morning not long after the funeral, I walk past Obst's garden and over the brick wall, through the wrought-iron fence, I see that long low mound of earth outside the Delaneys' dining room window that in every way resembles a long freshly filled grave. I know she is gone and buried, but I keep thinking about *maya*—that Hindu trope for the great mistake. You see a snake on the sidewalk and suddenly, almost at the same instant, realize it is no snake, but a crooked stick. We bumble around all day seeing snakes for sticks. (But just sometimes, isn't the snake really there?)

It sounds crazy, and Dr. Cobb won't approve, but for just the very shade of a second, I smile when I realize that I have mistaken the white shoots breaking the surface of Mr. Obst's loam for the slender, etiolated fingertips of Lydia Garrett Delaney.

About the Author

David Richard Belz was born in Baltimore's Union Memorial Hospital in February 1956, eleven days after H.L. Mencken died. He has been writing professionally for more than thirty years. As a Maryland State Arts Council literary competition finalist, he studied fiction writing with novelists James M. Cain and J.R. Salamanca at the University of Maryland in College Park. His essays, poetry, and fiction have appeared in such publications as *The Baltimore Examiner, The Baltimore Sun, The Evening Sun, City Paper,* the *Southern Literary Messenger, Oregon Review, Antietam Review, MacGuffin,* and *The Cynic.* He has been teaching writing since 1977. He graduated from Loyola College with a B.A. degree in English and Creative Writing and earned a master's degree in the Great Books from St. John's College in Annapolis as a National Endowment for the Humanities fellow. He lives with his wife and four children at the headwaters of the Jones Falls on Chestnut Ridge above the Greenspring Valley.

The future of publishing...today!

Apprentice House is the country's only campus-based, student-staffed book publishing company. Directed by professors and industry professionals, it is a nonprofit activity of the Communication Department at Loyola University Maryland.

Using state-of-the-art technology and an experiential learning model of education, Apprentice House publishes books in untraditional ways. This dual responsibility as publishers and educators creates an unprecedented collaborative environment among faculty and students, while teaching tomorrow's editors, designers, and marketers.

Outside of class, progress on book projects is carried forth by the AH Book Publishing Club, a co-curricular campus organization supported by Loyola University Maryland's Office of Student Activities.

Student Project Team for *White Asparagus:*
Sheila Watko, '12
Marguerite Pravata, '11
Lauren Hooper, '10

Eclectic and provocative, Apprentice House titles intend to entertain as well as spark dialogue on a variety of topics. Financial contributions to sustain the press's work are welcomed. Contributions are tax deductible to the fullest extent allowed by the IRS.

To learn more about Apprentice House books or to obtain submission guidelines, please visit www.ApprenticeHouse.com.

Apprentice House
Communication Department
Loyola University Maryland
4501 N. Charles Street
Baltimore, MD 21210
Ph: 410-617-5265 • Fax: 410-617-5040
info@apprenticehouse.com